Free Your Mind

Free Your Mind

◆

The Four Directions of an Awakened Life

Sensei Anthony Stultz

iUniverse, Inc.
New York Lincoln Shanghai

Free Your Mind
The Four Directions of an Awakened Life

iUniverse books may be ordered through booksellers or by contacting:

iUniverse
2021 Pine Lake Road, Suite 100
Lincoln, NE 68512
www.iuniverse.com
1-800-Authors (1-800-288-4677)

ISBN: 978-0-595-41953-1 (pbk)
ISBN: 978-0-595-86294-8 (ebk)

Printed in the United States of America

This book is dedicated to all beings who are seeking their True Self and to all those who helped me awaken to my own.

Contents

Preface

o o o o o o o o o o o o o o o o o o o o o o o o o o o o o o o o o
**All old truths want a new interpretation so that they can live
on in a new form.**

—Carl Jung

The book you are about to read is the culmination of a lifetime of my work helping people experience a positive transformation of their lives. I began my own
spiritual journey at a very young age. I was probably six or seven years old when I
first felt the call to be a minister. I was standing in the sacristy of a little Method-
ist church in New York when I had a mystical experience. It was then that I knew
I was destined to help others connect to the holy oneness at the center of life. My
early spiritual experience was in the Hebrew and Christian traditions of my parents. My fascination with ministry began when I was introduced to the powerful
preaching and charismatic fervor of the Evangelical Christian tradition.

At ten years old, I first heard of the Buddha through the popular television
show *Kung Fu*. I was deeply drawn to this mysterious Eastern path and the sub-
tleties of the martial arts. I began to read voraciously on the subject, everything
from Lao-tzu, Alan Watts, *The Dhammapada*, and Jack Kerouac to Bruce Lee's
philosophical works. My aunt, a native of Japan, was kind enough to share stories
of her own Buddhist practice and to explain what it was like growing up in a pre-
dominately Buddhist country. Emboldened, I sought teachers, and I eventually
began to practice in earnest what Buddhists call the Dharma.

Still unsure of how to best bring this message of liberation to others, I experi-
mented by becoming a minister in the Episcopal Church while leading meditation groups on the side. Eventually, I no longer felt comfortable teaching
Christianity. Before leaving for The Episcopal Divinity School and Harvard University in Cambridge, Massachusetts for my second round of graduate studies, I
had a powerful dream in which the Buddha Archetype of Compassion (Kanzeon)
beckoned me to teach.

Not long after settling in Cambridge, I began to lead a local Buddhist community. I sought ways to communicate the teachings of the Buddha to contemporary folks. I also served for a short while as the Buddhist chaplain to Japanese students at Harvard, and I was surprised to find that even though these students had been raised in the Dharma, they did not clearly understand the heart of the practices. I decided that a new way to present the teachings of the Buddha was required, and I slowly molded an approach that would speak to the hearts and minds of present-day people. I wanted to provide a method that allowed people to immediately understand and experience the power of the practices.

Ultimately I developed the Four Directions using the foundational practices and teachings of the Buddha, while integrating the insights of Western psychology. Naming the approach the Four Directions was inspired by the image of the mandala, or sacred circle, which is central to Buddhist iconography and a foundational understanding in the psychology of Carl Jung.

In 1997, I formed The Blue Mountain Lotus Society (www.bmls.org) as a medium for my students to explore and experience this novel approach to developing clarity of mind, openness of heart, and fullness of life. Discovering which methods and instruction worked for the people I helped ultimately shaped my style and formed the Four Directions method. It is a method that continues to grow and evolve as a unique branch of the Navayana School of Buddhism[1].

Sensei Anthony Stultz
Satori 2006

Introduction

○ ○

I grasped the life of the Buddha as the reality of the [True] Self which had broken through and laid claim to a personal life.

—Carl Jung

Buddhism is one of the oldest spiritual traditions in the world. It has transcended time and culture to surround the globe with the teachings of the Buddha and has permeated many cultures with a skillful combination of compassion and wisdom. Buddhism's growing popularity is an exciting development. One of the most prominent arenas for Buddhism's growth in the United States is through the integration of human services and what some scholars consider a new form of Buddhism, the Navayana School, which is primarily concerned with the social engagement of suffering in a variety of settings.

Sensei Anthony Stultz represents an influential movement of this new form. As a pioneer of Navayana Buddhism, he has devoted his life to sharing the teachings of the Buddha through the lens of contemporary society. After serving for more than twenty years as a teacher and pursuing ongoing study, he has become an expert in the art of healing. Combining a charismatic spirit with the insights of both Buddhism and Western psychology, he has created the Four Directions, a unique approach to relieving suffering. Born and raised in the United States, Sensei Stultz also represents a new generation of Buddhist teachers who bring East and West together in an exciting spiritual alchemy.

As a student and friend of Sensei Stultz for nearly fifteen years, I have had the honor and privilege of learning the Dharma from him not only in formal situations such as private counseling and seminary, but also in more intimate ways as an observer and participant in his life. I have witnessed Sensei Stultz share the Dharma with a roomful of hardened salesmen, and I have seen them awaken through his teachings. I have seen him serve at the bedside of the dying, minister to the blessing of a new birth, and engage in all that life offers in between. I have also been at his side on more than one occasion when he physically intervened to protect the welfare of another.

What is common among all of these experiences is that throughout each, his devotion to and skillful teaching of the Dharma resulted in the relief of suffering. His commitment to a life lived freely and fully underscores everything that he does, whether it is leading a retreat, cruising down the highway on his Harley Davidson, or smoking a cigar. Sensei Stultz embodies the Dharma not as something that he does but as something that lives through him.

We are blessed to be able to receive one of his unique contributions to helping people relieve suffering in *Free Your Mind*. As the title implies, Sensei Stultz offers here a new expression of the timeless teachings of the Buddha. Regardless of religious affiliation, political views, or lifestyle, *Free Your Mind* has something for all.

The first dialogue connecting Buddhism and America is often attributed to the discourses of William James, considered by many to be a father of Western psychology. In 1902, James was lecturing on psychology at Harvard University when a Buddhist monk and teacher named Dharmapala, the same teacher that taught at the World Parliament of Religions, entered the hall to listen to the lecture. James promptly invited him to take the head chair and teach his class. After Dharmapala finished teaching Buddhist doctrine, James referred to Buddhism as the psychology of the future.

James believed that Buddhism had the potential to make a substantial impact on America in two ways. First, he predicted an explosion in discourse on the relationship between Buddhism and psychology. Second, James implied there would be a great growth in the number of Buddhist practitioners in America.

Although James certainly brought the psychological impact of Buddhism to the fore in 1902, scholars often attribute Buddhism's first real voice in America to the Transcendentalist movement of the 1840s. The Transcendentalists, spearheaded by Henry David Thoreau, Walt Whitman, and Ralph Waldo Emerson, were among the first generation of Americans to have a relatively complete set of translated Buddhist texts. More than simply extrapolating from these texts, the Transcendentalists tugged at the imagination of a whole generation by challenging its blind acceptance of authority. This is a fundamental tenet in Buddhism that stood in stark contrast to the popular religion of the time, which preached one text as the single authority and truth.

Furthermore, Thoreau demonstrated that these Buddhist teachings were actually keenly in accord with the fundamental philosophy of an America experimenting with democracy. After all, the early Buddhist communities were among the first democratic societies. Buddhism offered an ideology that aligned with democratic values. The Transcendentalists had fertilized the American psyche to receive the Buddha's teachings on a grand scale.

One of the main avenues through which Buddhism has found root in contemporary American society is the practice of psychotherapy in particular and the field of human wellness in general. Whether the integration is through techniques that are used by psychotherapists and psychiatrists or through meditation and mindfulness practice, seminars, and teachers, Buddhism has allied itself with human service. This is not surprising when one considers that the spiritual and practical foundation of Buddhism is psychosocial engagement.

Sensei Stultz was born into this fertile ground, a ground ripe with opportunity for the growth of Buddhism but also in need of a radically new approach to vitalize the Dharma and popularize it into the American milieu. To do so, Sensei Stultz created a new application for the timeless teachings of Buddhist developmental theory and the subsequent psychological well-being that serves as one goal for practice. Each stage, or skandha, is directly related to the traditional stages of development and offers new insight that incorporates elements and information from clinical psychology. Not only does Sensei Stultz offer new penetrating ideas, he also skillfully introduces meditation and mindfulness techniques that are accessible to the novice as well as influential for the experienced practitioner.

By introducing the Four Directions, Sensei Stultz offers the insights from his training and experience as a new expression of the Dharma. The Four Directions represents an efficient and comprehensive vehicle for transforming one's life and experiencing freedom. This vehicle is exciting for both meditation practitioners as well as all who seek a full and free lifestyle. As it is clear to see in Sensei Stultz himself, it is the fruit of the practice that truly matters, and the Four Directions offers a path to this experience.

Serving as the founder and spiritual director of The Blue Mountain Lotus Society, Sensei Stultz has created an independent Buddhist community that utilizes the roots of the Buddhist tradition to promote freedom. As a model for this teaching, The Blue Mountain Lotus Society presents a unique and authentic approach to the Dharma. Through his work, Sensei Stultz and The Blue Mountain Lotus Society offer spiritual and psychological relief to thousands of beings and also prepare new leaders of the Dharma for tomorrow.

Free Your Mind offers a detailed account of the Four Directions by providing simple yet elegant practices, noble insight, and personal case reviews. Sensei Stultz has opened his practice and experience for all of us to embrace. This work serves as a handbook and guide for each of us as we encounter all of life, both in its wonderful and its difficult aspects. By studying and applying the techniques offered here, every person can realize his or her own individual and interconnected potential.

Osho Thomas J. Shaffer, MA
Order of the Dragonfly

Before Beginning

[The] Buddha saw the cosmogonic dignity of human consciousness.

—Carl Jung

The title of this book comes from what I believe to be the Buddha's central message: freedom. In The Blue Mountain Lotus Society tradition we call the Buddha *the Liberator* and his teachings the *Word of Liberation*.[2] The Buddha's message was one of freedom and compassion. His teachings and the experimental community that he founded, the *sangha*, drew people from diverse backgrounds and situations—male and female, prince and pauper, sage and criminal. They were all drawn to the Buddha's radical and life-transforming teachings. These were teachings the Buddha's students knew would not only create a spiritual revolution but would also begin to challenge the racist and misogynistic social system of the day.

The Four Directions is a presentation of this *Word of Liberation* for those of us living today. It is a unique way to practice the Buddha's teachings through which everyone, regardless of background or problem, can find peace of mind, personal empowerment to achieve goals, or a greater freedom in life. It is unique because it brings together methodically the ancient wisdom of the East and the psychological language of the West, thereby making it easier for people in contemporary society to understand the Dharma and put it into practice.

One of the most exciting things about the Four Directions approach to the teachings is that you can begin to experience positive changes within only a few weeks of starting. In the chapters that follow I will explain in great detail the application of each direction, but for now I would like to give you an overview of terms that will be very important.

The True Self: This term, the archetype (an image common to all human experience) of wholeness, refers to the part of us that is unchanging, no matter what happens in life. It was never born, and it will never die. It is the source of self-love, self-acceptance, self-esteem, and inner peace. Although during trying times in our lives we may have difficulty finding the peace and acceptance of the True Self, through the practices of the Four Directions we know they are always present, always accessible, and always complete. This is the source of our wisdom and compassion.

The Ego Self: This term, the archetype of our conditioned identity, refers to the part of us that is always changing. It changes and adapts to the expectations of others and the expectations that we have learned and placed upon ourselves. It is the source of self-judgment, whether positive or negative.

The Psyche: This term, the archetype of the mental world, is synonymous with the idea that our minds are organic, balance-seeking organisms.

The basic goals of the Four Directions are to teach us to:

Stop. Take time to let the Ego Self reconnect with the limitless power and free-flowing energy of the True Self.

Look. Reorient ourselves to the True Self in order to understand life more clearly and compassionately.

Listen. Allow the True Self to guide us and free up the uniqueness and creativity of the Ego Self.

As you read each chapter, make sure you take time to practice the exercises included and follow the steps in sequence. I have found that when using this approach to investigate the nature of mind, it is critical to maintain an order to aid in conscious awareness and not be overwhelmed by unconscious energy. Try to practice with another person, either a friend or counselor, so you can clarify the insights you will gain. You can also contact a trained Blue Mountain Lotus Society mindfulness counselor at www.bmls.org.

Chapter Summaries: A Second Look

Each chapter is summarized at its conclusion. This will make the ideas easier to remember and to reference when you begin implementing the practices.

The Living Mandala: Stories Along the Way

The Buddha once said, "Do not trust in a teaching because it is from a sacred book or because it comes from an esteemed lineage. Test all teachings for yourself as a goldsmith purifies his metal by fire."

I completely agree with this wisdom. Because of this, at the end of each chapter that highlights one of the Four Directions, I will share a true story with you that will dramatically illustrate what is possible with these mindfulness practices. Over the past three millennia these practices have been tried, tested, and found true. Read for yourself how each direction forms a part of a living mandala,[3] a sacred circle of wisdom and compassion.

Let us now begin a journey which starts at our true center, a journey that moves back and forth in an ever-awakening adventure of being and becoming. It is an adventure into freedom, the adventure of freeing your mind.

1

The Five Stages: How the Ego Self Came to Be

Before we explore the Four Directions, let us look at the basic theory the method uses to understand how we develop what we defined as the Ego Self.[4] This theory is called the Principle of Causal Origination. It will be a very powerful aid in understanding the context for the practice of meditation and mindfulness.

Each person evolves through five stages of development. The collective effects of the events in each stage condition us in particular ways.

The first stage is heredity. Heredity includes the genetic material we inherit from our parents and our ancestors. This first collection of traits is related to the development of our biological form. Much of who we are, from the way we look to the way we act and behave, is heavily influenced by our biological inheritance. It is very important that we understand this, especially if there is any predisposition to disease. When dealing with the psyche, it is also important to understand if there is a predisposition to anxiety or depression. This is a very important variable to bring into harmony as we attempt to achieve our overall goal of wholeness. For example, a person who suffers from manic depression may not experience the full benefit of the Four Directions without also using medication.

The second stage is related to the yin, or feminine, energy and the feelings, both emotional and physical, we have in our psyches. Feminine energy is primarily fostered during a person's early upbringing. It comes from the relationship one has with his or her biological mother or the person taking the role of the mother. This relationship begins at birth and continues all the way through the age of seven or eight. The mother's health and well-being while pregnant are important, as is the child's delivery and any issues which could affect the child's psyche, such as oxygen deprivation. The relationship also hinges on the state of the mother's psyche during this time. If the mother is depressed or anxious during this period, those traits can affect the child's feminine energy.

The third stage, beginning at the age of eight or nine and lasting through age twelve or thirteen, is the yang, or the masculine, stage. The yang energy generally refers to a person's father. However, I want to emphasize that we are talking about psychic energy. This energy does not necessarily come from the biological father or even a male. In the case of homosexual parents, the energy could come from the parental figure that carries more of the masculine energy in the relationship. This third stage of our species' evolutionary development, the stage where masculine energy seems to unfortunately dominate both genders, appears to be especially vital as individuals develop their perceptions of the outer world. Function, analyses, and intuition will dominate those perceptions. People whose fathers were abusive, were not present, or were not emotionally available during the third phase of growth find that most of their neurotic and troubling tendencies come from this stage.

The fourth stage is the environment that the person has grown up in and is now beginning to explore as an individual. This is the stage where we seek to develop an understanding of who we are in the world. Determining our place in the world includes weighing social status, philosophy, religion, location, political background, and economic status. These factors become critical at the fourth stage because the person is beginning to compare his or her place in the social system to the placement of his/her peers. This stage usually begins around age thirteen or fourteen and lasts into adulthood, usually reaching completion by age twenty-five. By coincidence or not, this is also about the same time the brain finishes growing. For many young adults this stage can produce angst and turmoil as they try to negotiate the tenuous expanse between the powerlessness of being a child and the responsibilities of an adult.

The fifth formation, the conscious development stage, is the final level of development. This stage begins to emerge in the late-third or early-fourth stage. The consciousness development stage is reached when a person has a very clear or distinct sense of identity. The person is able to say, "This is me, this is who I am." As we all know, there is plenty of time in the fourth stage when we question who we are and what we will do.

Together these five stages, or aggregates of conditioning, comprise an individual's personality. This is who we think we really are. This is called the Ego Self. To illustrate these concepts more clearly, let us examine an imaginary friend.

Joe

Joe is forty years old and is a very successful physician. He is married with two young children. He is a pillar of his suburban community and has built a home in the same town that he grew up in. He has recently taken over his father's medical practice.

Joe, either consciously or, most often, unconsciously, looks back over his five-stage history and says to himself, "This is who I am." If Joe is overly attached to the acceptance of the earlier stages, if he feels he really needed to be a doctor and his parents really believed he needed to be a doctor, then Joe may become heavily attached to being a doctor in order to feel OK. He may develop what we call an attachment complex to that version of his identity. His father is a doctor, and that is the only identity that his parents ever led him to believe was acceptable. Joe fulfills that goal, becomes a physician, and moves on into his life.

On the other hand, if Joe was not overly attached to the early stages and felt alienated by them, he may develop an aversion complex and want to try to establish the opposite or the antithesis of those early stages. He may decide to pursue his joy in working with engines and become an auto mechanic rather than a heart surgeon.

The Psychic Eruptions

What is interesting from the Four Directions perspective is that somewhere along the line, if we live long enough, we will experience one of four events that will cause an eruption in the psyche. This eruption will lead to a sort of reversal of the personality which will in turn lead us to begin to question the meaning of life.

A) **Relationships**. The first event is associated with relationships. The eruption that leads to questioning may begin as we enter into our very first mature relationship, a relationship that usually involves marriage or a serious commitment. The eruption can also be connected to the birth of a child. Indeed, even more than being involved in a permanent relationship, having a child serves as a likely trigger to an eruption.

B) **Aging**. A second potential cause of an eruption is experiencing the process of aging in oneself, friends, or family members. This eruption does not take place until later in life, when we begin to experience great change.

C) **Mortality**. A third trigger is experiencing personal illness or the death of someone close. Each of these experiences leads us to realize our mortality. This trigger is often so strong or traumatic that it can cause a severe eruption.

D) **Depression and anxiety**. The fourth cause of eruption comes when we reach a crisis state and find ourselves in a deep depression or saddled with terrible anxiety. In this situation, we often turn to some form of religious or social authority in search of absolutes that can lift us out of the gloom and calm the terrible panic.

There is an inherent observation within the Four Directions that our psyche is like an organic system that is always seeking to find its homeostasis point. This is a point where a system stays in equilibrium as its parts automatically compensate for environmental changes. An eruption and the questioning that flows from it are an opportunity for growth and rediscovering our True Self. We will discuss this further throughout the book.

Any issues we did not work through in our early life are going to come back to haunt us at some point because the psyche is seeking homeostasis. The psyche resembles a system that in many ways parallels the physical universe. The energy of the psyche transforms in a constant process from simple to complex forms and then back to simple. It goes through many changes, but the energy is never lost. The mind has a virtual self-correcting mechanism that returns it to homeostasis; this is what we call our True Self.

Let us return to Joe. Dr. Joe suddenly, seemingly out of nowhere, develops anxiety about aging and starts to feel trapped by his commitments. He begins to act out in ways that are contradictory to his usual personality.

Joe has just encountered an experience that led to an eruption. In the next phase, Joe will likely seek out distracting excitement and attempt to recapture aspects of his youth. He might have an affair or suddenly change jobs. We see this all the time, and we call it the mid-life crisis. Many people get so caught up in this stage that the decisions they make and the actions they take cause irreparable damage.

It is important for a person to find clarity, awareness, and self-realization during this stage. This is a vital opportunity. A person can view the eruption as a negative event, but from the Four Directions point of view these eruptions provide the best opportunities for a person to get in tune with what is really going on.

What about Joe? Joe is essentially going to develop an aversion complex. He will likely want to get away from all the things that he had growing up, the same things he was attached to because they once defined him as being OK. Where he was once a respected pillar in the community, he will now care less about that and more about what he wants. He will start to focus on the opposites of the things that previously defined him.

In many cases, individuals abruptly leave their families and their professions. We are all familiar with examples. It may be that the individual indeed needs to reevaluate his/her relationship or perhaps reconsider his/her vocational direction. This could lead to the end of a marriage or to a reinvigorated relationship. This could also lead to a new career or a renewed approach to a chosen vocation. We go through these experiences like we go through any crisis.

The experiences can be dangerous, but they also provide an opportunity for creativity and transformation. This is part of the process we follow to establish clarity and harmony in our lives. The Four Directions focuses on opportunity because trying to stop the danger that evolves from an eruption is a dead end. The energy is so strong because there is motivation within the psyche to find wholeness.

Our Basic Programming

How can understanding the five stages and how they relate to our development help us on a daily basis? All the conditioning of the Ego Self is united into what we might call our programming system. This is similar to the operating system of a computer. On a daily basis, that basic programming interacts with experiences to create thought patterns in our minds. Those thought patterns are hardened into beliefs, and those beliefs in turn create new thoughts which are based on the same process of conditioning. Those thoughts in turn create feelings, and behavior follows the feelings. Consequences then flow from behavior.

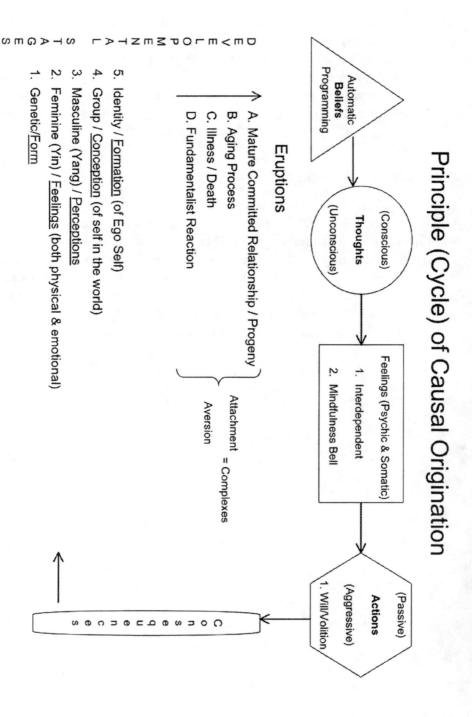

Principle (Cycle) of Causal Origination

Automatic
Beliefs
Programming

(Conscious)
Thoughts
(Unconscious)

Feelings (Psychic & Somatic)
1. Interdependent
2. Mindfulness Bell

(Passive)
Actions
(Aggressive)
1. Will/Volition

C
o
n
s
e
q
u
e
n
c
e
s

Eruptions

A. Mature Committed Relationship / Progeny
B. Aging Process
C. Illness / Death
D. Fundamentalist Reaction

Attachment
= Complexes
Aversion

D
E
V
E
L
O
P
M
E
N
T
A
L

S
T
A
G
E
S

5. Identity / Formation (of Ego Self)
4. Group / Conception (of self in the world)
3. Masculine (Yang) / Perceptions
2. Feminine (Yin) / Feelings (both physical & emotional)
1. Genetic/Form

You may not realize it, but you cannot have a feeling without first having a thought pattern to process. The trick is that a lot of our thoughts are so automatic and so deeply ingrained that they are often carried out unconsciously or subconsciously. As a result, they are also automatically processed. The process from thought to feeling is often so rapid that it seems we go directly into the feeling mode. We are often unaware of the thoughts that created the feelings which in turn create behavior or actions. The Four Directions practices can help us become aware of this process and enable us to take action, should we choose.

Behavior generally takes one of two forms, passive or aggressive. Whether a person chooses one over the other has a lot to do with nature and nurture, introverted and extroverted personality types, and the conditions involved. When a person behaves aggressively, he or she acts out based on feelings. When a person behaves passively, he or she is withdrawing from a feeling.

These actions in turn create consequences, the consequences lead to new thoughts, and the process is reinforced. The process keeps turning like a wheel. We call this the wheel of angst, uncertainty, or suffering. This wheel of suffering is endless, not only for the individual directly involved but for others as it is passed on to friends, associates, and especially to one's own children.

Negative conditioning patterns which begin with one particular person can be perpetuated for generations. The question that may arise at this point is, "What can we possibly do about this?"

The Process of Individuation

The answer from the Four Directions perspective is that we can begin to follow the psyche's inherent lure towards wholeness, or the True Self, and we can consciously guide the process. This is called individuation.[5] We can individuate, and we can become truly free of negative conditioning. We can learn clarity and understand not only where we come from but also what we need to do to obtain the freedom we so deeply desire. Our personalities, which are usually just conditioned masks or personas, become transformed into an awakened person through whom the True Self can be experienced and creatively expressed.

If we look through the five stages that lead to the Ego Self, we realize that the way many people depend on feelings to help determine who they are, what they should do, how they should act, or how they should interpret the actions of others is challenged by this practice that says a person cannot rely on feelings at all. Your feelings are never a good guide for how to act or how to think.

Feelings are dependent on thoughts for existence;[6] without thoughts, feelings would not exist. **The thoughts themselves are only creations of the mind and are not concrete entities.**

In terms of actions, behavior is largely about impulse, volition, or will. When I initially share the Four Directions with people, I do not devote much time in this area. Volition or will alone is not strong enough to completely change us or free us from conditioning. People who attempt new goals—losing weight, finding a new job, etc.—often fail. This failure is not due to a lack of will; rather, it can be attributed to the strength of the unrecognized conditioning.

In other words, we have plenty of willpower, but it is our thought processes that sabotage us. However, we can free ourselves from negative thought processes. The will to grow is built into us; we don't have to manufacture it. That will motivates us to begin a practice—like reading this book. For example, if I suddenly develop a craving for candy, I will usually focus on finding something sweet to eat rather than over-considering any obstacles to my confectionary satisfaction. However, when I am trying to lose weight, I might over focus on the obstacles. When we have difficulty, we only need a conscious act of determination to get us going again; our inherent will to grow will do the rest.

The Precepts and Hurt versus Harm

Let us return to the idea of consequences. If we remember the chain of our basic programming, all actions and choices have consequences. In the Four Directions, precepts are developed to help you consider and strategically minimize consequences. When working one-on-one, I use a version of the precepts[7] at the start of each person's practice. The precepts are not commandments because there is no punishment. They are also not absolute guidelines, but rather generalizations that help minimize consequences.

The first precept can be summed up by saying, "I will not intentionally cause harm to myself or to another." This is known as non-harming, and it means we have a new focus and understanding of the words "intention," "hurt," and "responsibility."

Let us look at the two levels of consequences. One level is the mundane level. For example, if I take billiard ball A and hit it into billiard ball B, physics and mathematics give me a good idea of what might happen. This is what we call cause and effect. The consequences are expected, and the reality of the situation is mundane.

However, what interests us here is something that is supra-mundane, the psychic aspect of cause and effect. Here we learn that we can only take responsibility for our intentions, not the outcome.

For example, Joe says something to Betty, and Betty becomes upset and hurt. Joe did not truly intend for his words to be hurtful, therefore Joe is not responsible for the situation. However, Joe could express responsibility for his actions by listening to Betty's feelings and empathizing with her. This exchange has the potential to expose their relationship to a clearer and more intimate mutuality. However, if Joe's intention is to cause Betty harm, it would be apparent that he is having difficulty within his psyche. In this situation he is working out of processes that are negative and destructive. In essence, what he is doing is trying to retaliate against his own negative conditioning by projecting it onto Betty. Projection is an important subject that I will discuss further in chapter three.

Intention is the main consideration, but we also need to understand that there is a great difference between hurt and harm. The reason I state in the first precept that, "I will not intentionally cause harm …," is that harm, from the point of view of this practice, is something that requires intention. If Joe intentionally upsets Betty and intentionally causes her harm, then there will be great psychic as well as mundane consequences.

Armed with the ability to differentiate between hurt and harm, we can begin to take responsibility for things that we have some control over, and we can let go of the things we cannot control. A surgeon who cuts into a person's body to remove a tumor causes hurt in order to heal. Maybe radiation or chemotherapy treatments follow. These may also cause hurt, but the intention of the surgeon is to heal and help.

Again, the first precept is, "I will not intentionally cause harm to myself or to another." Upholding this philosophy will minimize consequences. Next, I add, "… and to help others when I can." I have learned that intentionally seeking to help others achieve their fullest potential is the secret to my own fulfillment and happiness as an adult. However, people cannot forge toward intentionally helping others until they are aware of their own intentions. The practices of clarity and awareness you will find in the Four Directions are a vital foundation.

Comprehending human evolution and how problems develop is a basic component of the First Direction, which will be discussed in the next chapter. When I work one-on-one with an individual, we do not spend a lot of time revisiting the past. The past is the past, and our main concern is the present. However, the past does affect our present existence. For this reason, the past is discussed with regard to relationships in order to explore the total picture. Also, some people find that talking about their history or environment can be very helpful. Many have never shared their harmful historical experiences with another person. Exploring these experiences can be very powerful in terms of catharsis or release.

This purging can give a person a greater sense of motivation. However, according to our framework, this motivation cannot change a person fundamentally. In fact, delving into the past too much and stirring up memories without any direction can actually make a person's situation worse.

We also do not focus on feelings because feelings are dependent on thoughts. We do not focus on actions other than to engage our willpower or volition; nor do we focus on consequences other than to adopt the precepts to minimize negative consequences and attempt to slow down the wheel of cause and effect.

Our main focus will be on thoughts. First we will do this through meditation in terms of calm abiding, a period of quiet observation of the thoughts, feelings, and sensations that arise in the mind. We will then implement mindfulness in terms of clarity or insight into the origins of thoughts, feelings, and sensations. These methods are the keys to developing awareness, and awareness is our guide throughout the Four Directions.

Summing it up
The Five Stages: How the Ego Came to Be

- Each person is said to evolve through five stages of development. The events in each stage affect or condition us in particular ways. We carry this conditioning with us as we move through the process of life.

- The first stage is heredity. It includes the genetic material we inherit from our parents and our ancestors. The second stage is related to the yin, or feminine energy, and the feelings, both emotional and physical, we have in our psyches. The feminine energy is usually created primarily from the relationship we have with our biological mother or the person taking the role of the mother in our upbringing. The third stage, beginning at the age of eight or nine and lasting through age twelve or thirteen, is the yang, or masculine stage. It generally refers to our fathers, but it does not necessarily come from the biological father or a male. The fourth stage is the environment that the person has grown up in and is now beginning to explore as an individual. This is the stage where we seek to develop a conception of who we are in the world. This conception takes into account social status, philosophy, religion, political background, and economic status. The fifth aggregate, the conscious development stage, is the final level of development. The conscious development stage is reached when a person has a very clear or distinct sense of identity. At that point, they can say, "This is me; this is who I am." Together these five stages, or aggregates of conditioning, comprise an individual's personality, called the Ego Self.

- If a person lives long enough, he or she will experience one of four events that will cause an eruption of the psyche. The eruption will cause a sort of reversal of the person's personality which will in turn lead the person to begin to question the meaning of life. The first event is related to relationships. A second potential cause of an eruption is coming face-to-face with the process of aging. The third event includes experiencing personal illness or facing the death of someone close. During the fourth event we reach a crisis state and find ourselves in a deep depression or with terrible anxiety and we begin to seek an outer form of security.

- Any issues we did not work through in our early life are going to come back to haunt us at some point because the psyche is seeking homeostasis. The idea is that the psyche resembles a system that in many ways parallels the universe.

- All of the conditioning of the Ego Self is united into what we might call our programming system. On a daily basis that basic programming interacts with experiences to create thought patterns in our minds, and those thought patterns are hardened into beliefs. Those beliefs in turn create new thoughts which are based on the same process of conditioning. Those thoughts in turn create feelings, and then behavior follows the feeling. Behavior generally takes one of two forms, passive or aggressive. Whether a person chooses one over the other has a lot to do with nature and nurture, introverted and extroverted personality types, and the conditions involved. When a person behaves aggressively, he or she acts out based on feelings. When a person behaves passively, he or she is withdrawing from a feeling.

- Feelings are dependent on thoughts for existence. The thoughts themselves are creations of the mind and are not concrete entities. Behavior is largely about impulse, volition, or will.

- In the Four Directions, precepts are developed to help a practitioner consider and strategically minimize consequences. The first precept can be summed up simply as, "I will not intentionally cause harm to myself or to another." This is known as non-harming. Upholding this philosophy will minimize negative consequences. Next, I add "… and to help others when I can." I have learned that intentionally seeking to help others achieve their fullest potential is the secret to my own fulfillment and happiness as an adult.

2

The First Direction:
Rediscovering the True Self

Our first goal is to step back and obtain a clearer view of our thoughts and feelings. We will accomplish this by exploring each of the Four Directions, studying each step on its own, and using a model to illustrate. We will then apply those models to mental exercises. Together, this will allow you to cognitively and experientially grasp the basic ideas of the Four Directions so you can apply them in your own life.

Model 1: Self-Esteem vs. Self-Confidence

The first model used in the First Direction is the Self-Esteem versus Self-Confidence Model. Most people define self-esteem as the feelings they have about themselves or the feelings that others have about them. This reveals an unclear sense of what self-esteem is and where it comes from. To say self-esteem is a feeling is incorrect, yet we have all been programmed to believe this to be true. Why?

According to the Four Directions, we evolved from lower life forms into higher life forms. At some point in our evolutionary history, we became self-conscious creatures. As we became self-conscious creatures, all the survival instincts that brought us to the top of the food chain were integrated into the self-conscious psyche. We went from being in the realm of the animal world, where we were just another animal reacting to our environment, to being a self-conscious creature that could now begin to anticipate things, remember, and use those memories to create situations in the present.

That survival instinct in the genome (the genetic information inherited from our parents) has been transferred into the psyche and then mutated into a primal aspect of the Ego Self. Our self-defense mechanisms now include the survival of the ego rather than just the survival of the physical body.

Both survival instincts use the same basic defense mechanism. However, in beings whose brains have highly developed frontal lobes, the self-esteem mechanism becomes more complex. The model of self-esteem that I use asks people to question how we define the term self-esteem in order to help us redefine it.

Exercise 1: Defining Self-Esteem

In this exercise we will define the terms self-esteem and self-confidence for ourselves. First, look at the word "esteem." It is rooted in an economic term that means estimating. When we estimate something we are talking about its value or worth. Everything has a value or worth to us, but this depends on many factors. If I have a bronze plaque that someone I love gave to me and I am asked what its value is, there are many ways to estimate this. I can get it appraised, or I can go on eBay and find out what its market value is. However, to me, because of whom it came from and the relationship that it represents, its value is likely much, much greater than the monetary value others would put on it. Our consideration of self-esteem concerns what we believe our inherent value or worth is and how we come to that estimation.

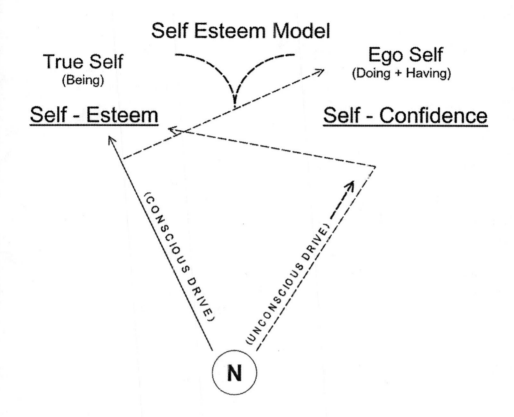

In order to understand this model more clearly, we separate this estimation into two categories, self-esteem and self-confidence. These are two worlds that coexist and yet are not the same. In the Four Directions we call this the relationship between the absolute and the relative. Self-esteem and self-confidence can be seen as two wings of one bird. We cannot escape from the world of experience, and we cannot ultimately hide from our experiences in some idealized concept of being. Both sides need to be understood and addressed.

In the model we put self-esteem on one side and self-confidence on the other. Self-confidence is the realm of feeling, doing, and having. We call this the Ego Self. Self-esteem concerns what we call the True Self, our essential being. The True Self is something inherent; it does not depend on what we have or do. The model thus has *Being* on the self-esteem side, while *Doing* and *Having* are on the self-confidence side.

When people define self-esteem as their feeling about themselves or the feelings that others have about them, this actually belongs in the realm of self-confidence. This comes as a big surprise to most people! The Four Directions practice takes the radical view that our being is, in essence, of a great inherent value which cannot be determined by doing and having, self-confidence or the Ego Self.

Remember, we are not talking about trying to get rid of one side while keeping the other. It is essential to understand that in an enlightened life, we have to integrate both.

Exercise 2

Let us say that on the self-esteem side, on a scale of one to ten, Joe has an inherent value of ten. This would be the numeric definition of the Ground of His Being. This number is always ten no matter what happens in Joe's life. The self-confidence side also incorporates a scale of one to ten, but a person's estimated level constantly moves between one extreme and the other. For example, if Joe feels good about himself because he became a doctor like his parents wanted, he might determine that his self-confidence level is approximately a nine. However, if he starts to question his decision to become a doctor and begins to behave in a way that people do not like, his self-confidence level is going to go down. If Joe is a young, strong, skilled surgeon, his confidence as a surgeon may be high—a nine. However, if he injures his hand or if as he ages his hands become weak or arthritic, his confidence may decrease substantially, perhaps to a two.

The realm of self-confidence is insatiable and unstable. It is constantly changing. The values applied during the self-confidence exercise are always going from one to ten and back. They are constantly changing. In contrast, the exercise suggests the idea that the being, or self-esteem side, never changes. It is not based on feelings or free association. Its value is constantly a ten.

Say that Joe finds a cure for cancer. His self-confidence measure will greatly increase. On the other hand, if this same cure later is found to have unfortunate and deadly side effects, his number on the self-confidence side is going to go down, while his self-esteem will remain a ten. The point to be driven home here is that **the self-esteem side never changes**. This allows Joe a constant ground from which to start over.

Next, let us imagine that we all are born with an inner compass that aids us in orientation and sets up a mental North. Because of the way we have evolved, our inner compass points first to doing and having to try to falsely achieve and maintain a sense of being. This has a many-fold effect, but two insights that arise are especially relevant.

The first insight: Anything we do begins, in our perception, to carry the weight of our entire being with it. Yet nothing we can do—relationship, job, status, talent—can carry the weight of our being. That is why those things fail to ultimately satisfy us; it is why people who have material possessions, good looks, success, and status can be just as depressed, anxious, and disturbed as anybody else.

The second insight: If we want to make changes to improve our self-confidence but we continuously are actually trying to improve our worth, we often fail to see the actual changes that we need to make to improve our performance. I love to tell folks about an interview I once read concerning Thomas Edison after he had created the first commercial light-bulb. The interviewer observed that the quest to find a commercial bulb had required 5,000 different experiments. He then asked Edison what it was like to fail 4,999 times. Edison, taken aback, said that he had honestly never looked at it that way. To him, experimentation was just a 5,000-step process.

Unfortunately, most people tend to do the opposite and adopt a less objective point of view. We may consider any mistakes we make to be fatal, and therefore we both ignore character flaws and continue to make the same errors, or we retreat into the false safety of not attempting anything that would truly challenge us and help us grow.

What we want to do in our new approach is shift the focus. We are not trying to get rid of the Ego Self. This is a vitally important point. A lot of philosophies and religions talk about the Ego Self as some terrible, negative concept. They preach that if we could only rid ourselves of our egos, then we would be OK. Frankly, the only people I have met who were without Ego Self were also clinically psychotic.

From a practice point of view, this understanding of the Ego Self/True Self dynamic ultimately leads us beyond a dichotomy. The absolute participates in the relative, the relative in the absolute. The True Self and Ego Self are interdependent. What we are talking about is a change of orientation, a change in direction. We are putting Ego Self into its harmonious and holistic perspective. We enable the shift by establishing the True North of our inner compass as the True Self.

By changing that orientation, by going to the True Self first for our understanding of being and then to the self-confidence world, two things happen. First, we can find happiness and wellness and then pursue individual goals. This is very different from a belief that if we achieve individual goals first, then we will be happy. We turn the whole thing upside down. For example, many people have studied psychologist Abraham Maslow and his hierarchy of needs pyramid. At the top of that pyramid is self-actualization. The ideal person has to have the appropriate shelter, education, status, etc., before achieving or being concerned with self-actualization. Unfortunately, in the Western world, your chances at obtaining all those things are greatest if you are male, white, of European descent, and lucky. If you are anything else, your chances are reduced.

The self-esteem model takes that pyramid and flips it upside down by teaching that you can experience a state of self-actualization first and then manifest all those other things as the True Self. The Four Directions offers people this fantastic notion. That is why it is so appealing and why so many people have found this approach to be very useful. It cuts across gender and cultural heritage, and it goes beyond all the dictates of the genome of survival.

A very easy way to look at this is to imagine that a young child is placed on your doorstep, and you assume responsibility for raising him or her. You can choose either self-esteem or a self-confidence orientation for the child. You can say, "You know what, Joe? Right now you're a ten, but let's see how you grow. Let's see how good-looking you become. Then we'll factor in how much intelligence and talent you possess."

If you take this approach, all these factors begin to create Joe's identity. He may become a nine on the self-confidence scale, or he may become a one. His outcome would depend on what criteria he is judged on. You could also say, "Joe, you are a one right now, but if you work really hard and do all the right things, you will eventually be a nine. But don't screw up or make any mistakes and make sure you get great grades."

On the other hand, you can nurture Joe by saying, "Joe, you, by being born, have an inherent value of self-esteem, and that value is a ten. That's as high as it can get. It will never go lower, no matter what you do or have. You will always be a ten."

Which orientation do you think is more likely to lead Joe to grow into an adult who is generally happy, has a sense of well-being, sees life as an adventure, and can find positive, creative ways to deal with his problems? The answer is obvious. Anybody who is shown this model, whether they are corporate executives or teenagers, looks at it and answers, "Of course, the self-esteem orientation."

Again, that is not how we have been genetically predisposed. Why is that? It is because we are still largely acting as unconscious beings. Primitive conditioning has programmed us like robots to survive at any expense and to get to the top of the food chain. This creates what we call the egocentric, or selfish, personality.

We do not have to live like this. Paradoxically, self-consciousness not only brought egocentricity to the psyche, but it also can help us find freedom, liberation and have real, lasting happiness. We can choose to live by the Self-Esteem Model.

Model 2: Wholeness versus Perfection

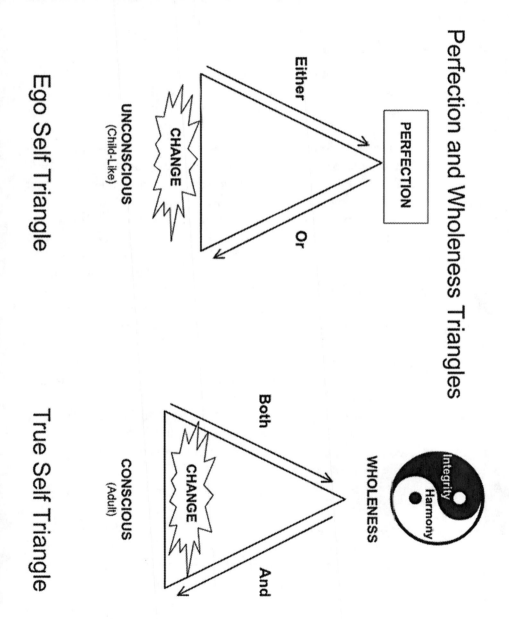

Another way to picture how differently the world is viewed through the Ego Self and through the True Self is the Wholeness versus Perfection Model. This model has two triangles. One triangle represents the Ego Self and its unconscious pursuit of perfection, while the other triangle is based on the True Self, or the conscious aspiration for wholeness.

The Perfection Triangle

The Ego Self side has a triangle with a rectangle at the top. The word "perfection" is in that rectangle; this illustrates that perfection is the goal when we're dealing with the Ego Self. The orientation of the Ego Self is an unconscious attempt to try to achieve perfection.

From the Four Directions perspective, perfection is a delusion. It never existed, and it never will exist. There is terrible fallout from pursuing perfection: we see the world in black-and-white. Most of us have been conditioned to look at the world as actually being perfect or imperfect. Because we are seeking perfection, we believe that it exists. I challenge people to give me an example of something in this world that is literally perfect. Can you? This view is a delusion that distorts how we look at life and how we deal with life experiences.

Outside of and below the Ego Self triangle is the word "change" with danger zigzags surrounding it. Change is seen as the enemy because we either try to change things to obtain some sense of perfection, or we try to prevent things from changing so we can also prevent losing the perfection we believe we have achieved.

We need a new model when an old model stops working for us. If we fail to replace it with a working model, there is no foundation for the psyche to use. When the psyche gets into trouble, it uses whatever model is available, even if it is an unhealthy one. This perfection model has been instilled in each of us for a long time. It has evolved for untold millennia. We cannot pretend that the solution is just to get rid of it. Science tells us that nature abhors a vacuum. This is just as true for the psyche as it is for the universe.

The Wholeness Triangle

We need to develop a new model, one that is based on the True Self. We still try to pursue things. That is the way we are made. However, change is no longer outside of the triangle of our life; it has been integrated. It is no longer seen as the enemy. It is opportunity. It is the opportunity to be creative and do something new.

The goal at the top of the True Self triangle is not perfection, it is wholeness, and we put a circle around it rather than a rectangle. The circle represents a home for our new goal of wholeness. We all inherently know we are drawn to wholeness. The yin-yang symbol represents this. Yang represents integrity, and yin represents harmony.

Integrity[8] means that I can integrate everything in my life: the good, the bad, and the ugly. I can integrate all of it into one. Every part has a place. I do not push any of the difficult or dark stuff away. I do not have a Pollyanna-like view. I see reality as it is, and I can integrate all my experiences. This process is about clarity, not about any particular philosophy of negativism or positivism, pessimism or optimism. There is the paradoxical riddle of a glass that is half empty to a pessimist and half full to an optimist. Our practice says that it is just a glass of water. Because our practice is about clarity, we can choose what we want to emphasize. We decide whether the universe is for or against us.

Our practice is also about empowerment. We are free to make choices and decisions about who we are and what our reality is. I can mold my life any way I wish. My life becomes my art. What a radical idea!

The yin symbol, harmony, means you can find a way to harmonize all aspects of your life, and the yang symbol means that you can integrate those aspects in a way that is well-balanced and fosters a view of life as a creative gift. The pursuit of this goal leads to a "both/and" attitude, meaning that you can include seemingly opposed forces in your life. The world becomes, as it is, both this and that. The world can be beautiful and wonderful and also ugly and terrible. People can be wonderful and compassionate, and they can be horrible and destructive, too. The reality is that good and bad coexist.

Exercise 3

This exercise, Reorientation Meditation, is the first meditation practice. We do this through a very powerful, successful, and subtle technique. When we are growing up through the five stages, most of our conditioning takes place in a pre-cognitive, pre-contextual manner, before a fully developed ego identity forms. During reorientation I use many of the insights from innovative educators such as Jean Piaget and Maria Montessori. We see the developing being as a sponge. Material is absorbed on a sub-cognitive level, or a sensual level.

The Centering Space

A. Centering Object
B. Stand or Altar
C. Incense and Incense Bowl
D. Candle
E. Flower with Vase
F. Water Bowl
G. Bell

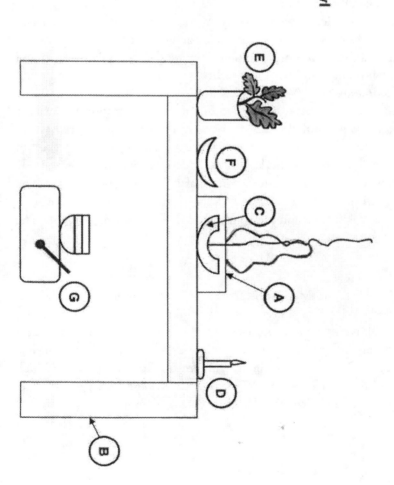

To start your reorientation, you create and establish a centering space (please see example). This is an actual physical space in which you place certain elements. In the center is an object that, to you, represents wholeness. It can be anything, but it must personally resonate with you. I like to use circular shapes because I believe that circles are nature's inherent way of pointing us to wholeness. This central object represents the True Self (in Buddhist temples you may see a Buddha used as the central object; this does not represent a person, but rather, an aspect of the True Self).

Place a candle on the right side. The candle represents that this exercise is not a one-time practice. You must relight the candle each time you practice. This is an observation that you choose to do every day. You cannot do it once and then forget about it. The flame itself symbolizes the light of enlightenment.

On the left, place a flower in a vase. The life cycle of the flower is a natural process. It communicates to us visually that everything is beautiful, everything is impermanent, and everything goes through changes. As the flower wilts and dies, we know its beauty is passing, and we replace it with a new one.

Set out a bowl of water. Water is a very powerful symbol of healing, purity, and clarity. I often use images like the still calm of a pond, or talk about things flowing like water. Water is an ancient symbol of healing.

Next, use a bell of some sort. The ring of the bell calls us to wholeness, the basis of the True Self. It is the voice of our True Self calling the Ego Self home.

I also recommend the use of incense, which we will light from the candle. We learn to see the incense as a metaphor for our daily practice. We allow its fragrance and essence to permeate our most primal sense, our sense of smell. The incense represents our giving back to the universe in a mindful way that leaves the perfume of an examined life that is lived freely and fully. Long after we are gone from the stage of this drama, the way in which we lived our lives will continue in the environment of the lives that we have touched.

Lastly, what we want to do is put our hands together, bow, and say to ourselves, "I take refuge in my True Self." We will say this every morning and every evening.

By performing these physical actions, we tap into the primal stages. However, this time, instead of someone else conditioning us, we are doing it for ourselves. We are finally in charge of our destiny.

When you get up in the morning, you should first bow in the direction of the centering space you've created. See it, take it in, and then go on your way to shower, brush your teeth, and prepare for your day. But make sure your first priority each morning is to acknowledge your centering space. At night, after you read, watch a movie, or make love, but before you go to sleep, again take refuge in the knowledge that this is the Ground of your Being. This is the source of all wisdom, compassion, and happiness. Whatever happened in that day, this is still your true source. Some people ask me if it is really necessary to acknowledge the centering space every day; I tell them that they should only do so as often as they practice physical hygiene. This acknowledgement should be considered a form of mental hygiene.

Most people find it useful to light the candle, light the incense, and ring the bell. Do whatever you feel is necessary. Experiment and find what works best for you.

In addition, take at least ten to twenty minutes to go over the models. Contemplate them constantly so you know the models by heart.

Test the models within your experience. The most important thing about this practice is finding what works for you.

I suggest that you keep a journal and use a number system to evaluate yourself. Every day at the beginning or the end, it does not really matter which, assign yourself a number from one to ten describing how you are feeling and write this in your journal. Try to use the first number that pops into your head. In psychology, this is called free association. It will help you get past the ego's defenses. Free association is typically what we do when we're dreaming, daydreaming, and fantasizing. This number provides a way for you to track the progress of your moods as you practice. It also helps to alert you to circumstances that may ignite certain feelings.

Can we trust our feelings? Here we do not trust our feelings; we are instead utilizing our feelings as a mindfulness bell, as a way to begin to understand what's going on inside us.

Using this approach allows us to begin to see that our feelings are changing, and what is changing our feelings is not our environmental situation; it is not our past; it is not our future. What is changing is the way we think. I always suggest that people journal. Writing things down or talking about them changes the way the brain processes our feelings. It really allows us to look at things in a whole new light.

Exercise 4

In this exercise we want to develop a way to allow the Ego Self to deeply relax. This can be accomplished through almost any activity that a person finds mentally and physically relaxing. However, the two activities I recommend most are sauntering and sitting still.

Sauntering involves taking a walk for ten to twenty minutes a day, with no goal or destination. That's it.

Sitting simply involves taking time to find a comfortable place to sit quietly for ten to twenty minutes while you either recite the mantra, "I take refuge in my True Self," or pay attention to the body's breathing. You can run an object, such as a mala or meditation beads, through your fingers. You can find an object to fix your gaze on, like a spot on a wall or your centering space.

While you sit, if a thought, feeling, or physical sensation arises, acknowledge it briefly, take a deep breath, and continue. The point of this exercise is not to push your thoughts, feelings, and sensations away but to not give in to them. One helpful method is to imagine your thoughts, feelings, and sensations as clouds passing through the open and spacious sky of your awareness. Some are dark and filled with rain, and some are white and filled with light. They are only temporary. Just watch them pass by.

Another method is to sit quietly and listen to the sounds around you. As you experience the sounds, you realize that they can affect your emotional status. A loud bang can make you feel anxiety; a soft hum can make you feel relaxed. You do not usually identify with the sound itself; rather you recognize that it is an object of your senses. However, we tend to associate thoughts as subjects. We identify thoughts as somehow being less objective, and we accept the delusion that our thoughts are who we are. However, just as the sounds I hear do not define me, neither do my thoughts. By taking part in this practice daily, you begin to allow your Ego Self to relax into the embrace of your True Self, which is always serene and peaceful. This practice will gently prepare you to begin making inquiries into the nature of your Ego Self conditioning, which you will learn about in Chapter Three.

Summing It Up
The First Direction: Rediscovering the True Self

- Self-esteem and self-confidence are two worlds that coexist and yet are not the same. Self-confidence is the realm of feeling, doing, and having. Self-esteem concerns what we call the True Self, or our essential being. We enable the shift from Ego Self to True Self by establishing the True Self as the True North of our inner compass.

- Perfection is an unattainable illusion, whereas wholeness emphasizes inclusion and happiness.

The Living Mandala: The First Direction, Ray

The First Direction practice of Reorientation is illustrated in this first story. When we reorient, we move away from the Ego Self as our center and toward the True Self as our center. This allows the Ego Self to relax into the embrace of the True Self.

The story that I like to use to illustrate Reorientation is the story of Ray. Ray is a fellow I got to know when I was running a halfway house in Johnstown, a small city in western Pennsylvania.

I had put together an idea for a halfway house after conducting meditation programs in state and federal prisons. While talking with a prison psychologist, I asked if there was anything I could do besides meditation and mindfulness counseling to help these prisoners.

She replied that a lot of inmates sentenced for non-violent offenses could get out of prison on good behavior if they had a family member or somebody on the outside willing to take an interest in them. The outsider would have to be willing to give the prisoner a place to stay until he could get back on his feet. However, many of these prisoners had no one. They were stuck doing the maximum time they'd been sentenced to unless someone from the outside world was willing to vouch for them. The psychologist said the creation of a halfway house would provide some of these men with a surrogate community, and the community could serve as an aid as the men attempted to transition their way back into the real world.

I went right to work and was able to get a couple of business people interested in the idea. My father and his partner put the money together, and we bought a house in the downtown area. We worked with the state prison system and established an independent halfway house. There were ten apartments in the building. The men lived there and were required to see me several days a week for counseling. There were also other requirements they had to fulfill, such as getting a job, continuing education, or attending drug and alcohol counseling.

One of the first ten men to enter the halfway house was a fellow by the name of Ray. Ray was in his sixties, and he had spent most of his life in prison. He was finishing a stint of almost twenty years when he came to my attention. I myself was only in my late twenties. Ray was a really interesting guy. His character reminded me of an aging Clint Eastwood. He was very cool, very quiet, and he spoke with a raspy voice. He had been a professional thief all his life, but he had never done anything violent, and he never carried a weapon.

After leaving prison, Ray took a bus directly to the halfway house, and I took him in. He had a hard side to him, as you can imagine of anyone who had spent so much time in prison. When Ray arrived at our house I interviewed him and gave him a room. The very next day, one of the men who had been at the house for awhile came to my office and said that Ray had threatened his life. Ray had taken a big bowie knife he'd purchased at a sporting goods store and stuck it in his neighbor's doorjamb. Ray threatened him with bodily harm if he didn't turn his radio off or stop playing it so loudly.

That was my first experience with Ray, and of course, I had to talk to him about it immediately. I left a note on his door telling him to come see me that day in my office. After he arrived, I explained to him that threats would not be accepted. He started to give me some grief about it. I was very straight with him and said, "Look, I will not tolerate violence or threats of any kind in this house. If you don't like it, fine, go back to prison, but I'm not having it here." I was pretty hard with him about it. I felt awkward about addressing him that way, because he was so much older than I was. However, I think I impressed him because I was not afraid of him or put off by his demeanor.

He never gave me any trouble after that, except once when a young Hispanic man came to the halfway house. He was much younger than Ray. Typically, the younger guys were a bit more aggressive and less respectful. The older residents tended to respect each other's space and leave each other alone.

Ray came to my office and said, "I'm not going to share any space with no goddamn spic. I didn't want to in prison, and I'm not doing it here."

I said, "Well, let me ask you something. How would you like me to treat you? Do you want me to treat you based on who people think you are because of your background, or would you prefer that I treat you based on my actual experiences with you?" He didn't say anything.

I continued, "Well then, I want you to extend the same courtesy to these fellows. You don't know them. I want you to try to base your thoughts about them only on your experiences with them and try to let go of who you think they are because of where they come from or the color of their skin." I again told him that I would not tolerate that kind of racist behavior at the house; everybody there got an equal start. I could tell that Ray wasn't happy, but he nodded in agreement and silently slid out of my office.

Ray was not a religious man, but he knew I was a meditation and mindfulness teacher. His curiosity was piqued, and he began to ask questions about the practices. He and I started to practice not just the counseling aspect but also meditation. One of the main practices I talked about with Ray was this idea of

Reorientation. Ray started to practice Reorientation. It became his main custom; he set up his altar space, placed an object at the center representing his True Self, and started to bow to that part of himself. Ray started to reorient and recognize that his center was coming from his True Self and not from his Ego Self.

Ray really took to the practice. I don't know if it was because of his age, having a need, or having nothing to lose. But here was this guy in his sixties who had never had any kind of exposure to this way of thinking before, working with this young twenty-something, who was still a little bit wet behind the ears, and we really connected. He really took to these teachings, and I saw a transformation take place that was really miraculous. He went from being a hard-nosed, squinty-eyed, don't-trust-anybody, everybody's-a-son-of-a-bitch guy, to a model for the rest of the residents in the house.

I began to recognize the way prison had shaped Ray. When you're in prison you live in a very small room, and space becomes very important to you. For Ray, that meant that when you came to his door, you took off your shoes. His room was immaculate, and he wore very simple clothes. He wore dungarees, a white T-shirt, and a blue jean jacket almost every day. On occasion, we would go to breakfast together, and he would always take his time. Sometimes I would find him shaving. Even the way he took care of his toiletries and shaving implements was done with great attention. He used an old-fashioned shaving brush. I can still remember the scent.

There was something always clean and clear about Ray, and when he combined it with his practice of Reorientation Meditation it seemed like all these little things came together. For example, during lunches at the corner diner he would always get a cheeseburger and a cup of black coffee. He would unwrap the burger and put everything neatly in its place. He would very mindfully take time to eat, and when he was eating he wouldn't speak. He would listen to me talk, but he wouldn't speak while he was eating. After he had finished a bite and taken a drink, then maybe he would say something. It reminded me of the mindfulness admonition, "When you eat, just eat."

He learned all these little things while living in prison. All these little things, which for some people may not be very significant, became manifestations of Ray's True Self. It was as if I was witnessing an old Zen monk come to life.

Eventually, I began to give Ray more responsibility. I saw that he was a natural leader, and I needed someone with that trait to keep order at the house. I made him the caretaker. He would report to me on different problems and things that needed to be taken care of, like basic carpentry. As time passed, we became very close. He had a real zest for life as evidenced by the fact that at sixty-seven years of age he met and dated a younger woman who could not have been much older than I was.

He was a very vigorous guy, and I grew to love him very much. Unfortunately, I did not know he had a heart condition. I'm not sure that he knew. One day he didn't show up for our morning meeting. I went over to the house, which was only a block or two from my office. I knocked on the door, but no one answered. Usually I'd smell his aftershave or the soap from his shower, but I couldn't smell anything. Because I had keys to all the rooms, I opened the door. He was lying face down on the bed. He had died of a heart attack. I remember being very saddened by that experience. At the same time, I remember seeing the body and thinking that that body was not him. His spirit was much bigger than his temporary self, and he'd simply outgrown his old form.

He had friends—older people and street people he'd taken care of—in that small city that the halfway house called home. He had given directions to one of his friends that he wanted to be cremated and that he wanted me to preside over his funeral. His wishes were respected, and the ceremony was beautiful. It was attended by homeless people and friends who lived downtown near the halfway house. About ten or twelve of us gathered and talked about Ray. I gave everybody the opportunity to say what Ray meant to them, and I shared with them what he meant to me.

One of the older women Ray had befriended approached me after the service was over and we had scattered his ashes at the river. She told me that Ray had really grown to love me. He felt as if I were the son he never really had. He and Israel, his biological son, had always been geographically and emotionally distant from each other. They had never really known each other. She said that Ray was so proud of who I was, almost as if he was my father. I remember writing letters to Ray's son, who was also in prison, and to his daughter-in-law and granddaughter. I informed them that Ray had passed away, and I made sure that they knew what kind of man he had become.

I frequently think of old Ray and how much he taught me. He showed me that your age, where you come from, or what you experience doesn't matter. Everyone can change, because none of our identities is fixed. Ray became who he always had been deep down inside, and his True Self really shined through.

3

The Second Direction:
Understanding the Ego Self

In this chapter we are going to dive deeply into a proposed structure of the psyche. In the following models and exercises we will learn to analyze our thought patterns so that we may gain an inner locus of control and communication.

Model 3: The Parent/Adult/Child (PAC)

Our next model, the Parent/Adult/Child Model, is very familiar in Western psychology. It focuses on different states of the Ego Self. There are three ego states, traditionally called the parent, the adult, and the child. In this practice, the first state, the parent, does not necessarily just represent our biological parents but represents the whole five-stage historical development. We use the word "parent" to recognize that this is the old stuff, the original conditioning, the archaic programming.

Again, we realize that there is a yin and yang to everything. The parent conditioning has two faces. One side of the parent, the yin side, is nurturing. It is very creative, positive, and loving. The other side, yang, is the critical and destructive aspect of the parent.

In turn, this creates an inner child with two faces or two aspects. The key to understanding the child is knowing that the child is the realm of the affective, or emotional, and somatic, or physical, expression of our Being.

The first part of the child is what we call the natural child. The natural child naturally flowers or grows under the nurturing of the yin side of the parent. There are certain traits that earmark the natural child, such as a sense of happiness, freedom, and well-being. The natural child has an inherent sense of, "I am OK," is comfortable in terms of his/her sexuality, and has a general sense of physical health and vigor. The natural child also displays a strong sense of humor.

In turn, the destructive or critical side of the parent creates in us the adapted or hurt child. This child had to adapt to all the parent's negative criticism and conditioning. The earmarks of that child generally are indicative of a person who is not well. Mentally, he/she is often depressed or very anxious. Physically, there is a lot of sickness and a lack of vigor or vitality. In the adapted child, there is sarcasm in place of a sense of humor. In sexual expression there is either frigidity or promiscuity. The adapted child surrounds itself with a wall of defense mechanisms to try to survive the criticism and the negativity of the parent. The problem is that the defense mechanisms were created by an innocent child as an unconscious means of survival, yet the world around us has changed, and we are no longer children.

The adapted child in us is not only related to our primitive evolutionary beginning as an individual, but also to our entire evolutionary history as a species. Fight-or-flight responses are related to this defense mechanism which usually takes on one of these two aspects with regard to reaction. Do you remember the model of the five stages and the discussion about will or volition? In this case, if we choose to fight, we strike out at the critical parent. The ultimate example of striking out against that negative conditioning is homicide. While working in prisons, I discovered that many people who engage in violent behavior are really trying to attack that conditioning.

If we choose the flight mode, we withdraw or dissociate from the critical parent. The ultimate expression of this is when people try to destroy themselves with either slow (addiction) or immediate suicide. However, the person projects the expression onto something else because his or her need for acceptance from the object of the projection—the inner child's need for the parent—is too great.

Parent, Adult, Child

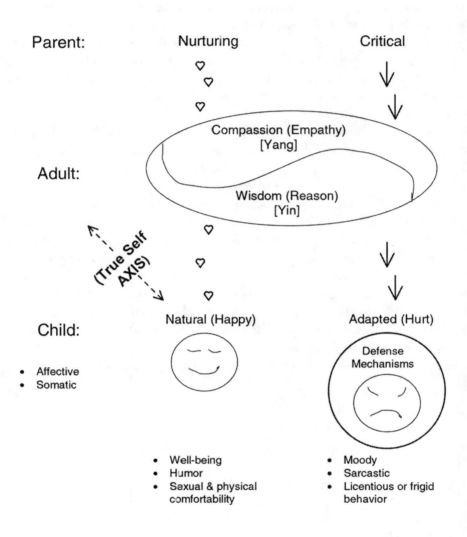

Parent: Nurturing   Critical

Adult:

Compassion (Empathy)
[Yang]

Wisdom (Reason)
[Yin]

(True Self AXIS)

Child: Natural (Happy)   Adapted (Hurt)

- Affective
- Somatic

Defense
Mechanisms

- Well-being
- Humor
- Sexual & physical
  comfortability

- Moody
- Sarcastic
- Licentious or frigid
  behavior

Exercise 5

Let us return now to Joe. Joe's uncle used to abuse him sexually. Joe will often act out the same way toward another person, thus projecting the energy from his uncle. What he is really trying to do is to reconcile his aggression and fear.

For example, if Joe found the sexual experience to be pleasurable, but as a child had no cognitive context or conceptuality, then he may as a young adult become promiscuous. If he found the experience disturbing, then as a young adult he will probably withdraw from physical contact and be very confused about his sexuality.

The other extreme, passive action or behavior is to try to do things to gain the sympathy and attention of the parent and to try to revert back to a dependent state. This is where we see a lot of drug addiction and other addictive behaviors. The ultimate experience of trying to escape the parent is suicide. That is how powerful this relationship conditioning is.

In the middle we have our saving grace, our conduit from the ego to the True Self, and that is what we call the adult. The adult is the intermediary between the parent and the child. It represents a person who is awake. The adult also has two parts, a yang and yin aspect. The yang aspect is compassion. The adult in us knows how to be empathetic; it knows how to be compassionate. Secondly, the adult in us knows how to reason because it has wisdom, the yin aspect.

One of the things we do in the mindfulness approach is to give ourselves time for the adult to come on board as we meditate and reorient ourselves. In the diagram of the psyche that I use, I put a captain's chair in the center of a circle representing the psyche. For most people the parent is sitting in the captain's chair, and underneath the chair is the adapted child. Behind the chair, poking its head out every now and then, is the adult.

(Parent/Adult/Child) Captain's Chair Model
Original Model

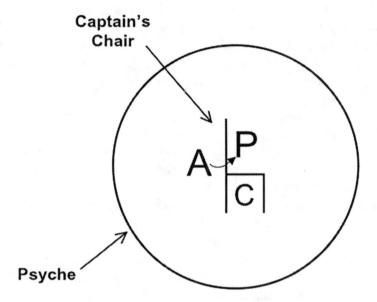

**Captain's
Chair**

Psyche

We now want to create a new diagram. Our new diagram has the adult sitting in the captain's chair of the psyche; the critical parent is put under the chair; and the natural child is set free under the protection and supervision of the adult.

It is wise to differentiate between the two models. But once again, we are not getting rid of anything. We are integrating everything while changing orientation. It is the psychic application of the Chinese idea of feng shui, which refers to finding harmonious placement.

(Parent/Adult/Child) Captain's Chair Model
New Model

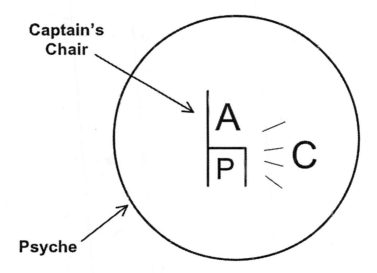

How does this work? The meditation exercise we learned in Chapter 2 gives the adult time to come aboard and get into the chair. The first thing the adult offers is compassion toward our own inner child, because that child is not going to be set free until it feels love and safety. We can do this for ourselves. We can become our own best friend and our own best companion by first and always offering compassion to that hurt part of us. When the child in us feels safe we can offer wisdom and reason. However, if we try to reason with the child without allowing it to express itself, without allowing it to feel secure, it will put up its defenses.

Exercise 6

The Parent/Adult/Child Model offers us a new language that I often use in relationship work. When we tried Exercise Four we began to see what practicing sitting meditation can do for us. While we are meditating and observing our thoughts, we then add the process of labeling where a thought or feeling comes from so we can see whether its source is the parent, the adult, or the child.

We begin this labeling practice with sitting meditation, and it is very simple. Find a time during the day where you can sit for at least ten minutes, but no more than twenty minutes. You can usually combine this practice with one of your periods of Reorientation practice. While sitting, I want you to simply use your breath. Either watch or count each breath from one to ten, then start again with one. You can also use a repetitive word or a mantra—a syllabic word-sound—that you have been using in Reorientation. Then let your mind do what it does. You have to sit quietly to give yourself a chance to listen. That's an important part of this practice. Sometimes you may be a little agitated. At those times it is good to saunter or do some moving meditation: tai chi, yoga, etc., before you sit.

When a good thought arises, you do not want to become too attached to it. You also do not want to develop any aversions if a nasty thought comes into your mind. You want to let the thought be, and then to go back to focusing on the breath. Again, if a pleasant or unpleasant physical sensation arises you do not want to be too attached to or averted from it.

You want to develop a strong sense of acceptance during your sitting. Maybe a feeling comes up that is really strong. Remember to just let it pass, neither hold onto it nor reject it. The point is that you want to accept all that you feel. If you are being drawn in or being pushed away by a thought, a feeling, or a sensation, you simply want to return to your breathing, stabilize yourself, and bring yourself back to the present moment. Those thoughts and feelings will try to drag you into the past or push you into the future. By learning to identify with your aware-ness you can learn to live in the present moment, or what some call the eternal now.

The next part of this practice is to simply label a thought as a thought when one arises. Tell yourself, "I'm having a thought." When you feel something, say to yourself, "I'm having a feeling." If you have a physical sensation, you can say, "I'm having physical sensation." The purpose is to recognize that you are starting to associate with your awareness rather than your thoughts and feelings, and you are starting to use language differently. You are not sad; you are *feeling sad*. You are not depressed; you are *feeling depressed*. You are simply being, not doing and having.

As you become more comfortable with this practice, you can begin to look at the process in terms of the parent, the adult, and the child. You can say, "I'm having a thought that is coming from my parent," or "I'm having a feeling that's coming from the hurt child." Then go back to the breath.

For example, you are sitting there and suddenly you think, "That person really does not like me, but I should not think that way." You are having two thoughts. The first thought is, "That person really does not like me." The second thought is, "But I should not think that way." Using the model you realize that the first thought is coming from the hurt child. The second thought is coming from the angry parent. You can also use time and say that the thought is coming from the past or the future. The adult thought is always in the present.

It is a very simple and easy practice, but it does take effort and repetition. Soon you can train yourself to think with clarity while remaining focused and in the present. What we are engaged in is discipline, which simply means self-guidance. This differs from a habit, because a habit is a combination of conditioning and exposure. For example, no child has to learn to like sugar. One try and the child is hooked for life. This is because our ancient ancestors discovered sugar in fruits, and a strong reaction to it is now built into us. However, learning to balance one's consumption of sugar is a demonstration of discipline.

Labeling and Observing

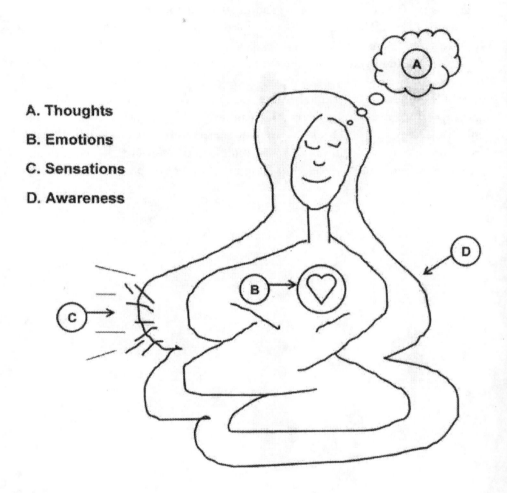

A. Thoughts

B. Emotions

C. Sensations

D. Awareness

Exercise 7

This exercise includes two techniques. In Technique One, two people sit facing each other, with one playing the Ego Self voice while the other person plays the voice of the person's True Self. It is important that we remember that the True Self always begins with compassion, and then moves into wisdom. Whenever the Ego Self voice gets stuck or can't respond, the True Self begins to guide it toward clarity.

Here is a verbatim example:

> Ego Self: *You're an idiot and a loser. You'll never be happy.*
> True Self: *Please tell me more.*
> ES: *What more do you need? You just don't count!*
> TS: *That is exactly how I feel.*
> ES: *Who cares what you feel?*
> TS: *I do.*
> ES: *Why do you care?*
> TS: *I'm not sure. What do you think?*
> (At this point the Ego Self voice faltered and began to search for a response.)
> TS: *Please, I really do want to know.*
> ES: *(Begins to let down its defenses and speak of its pain.)*

When this breakdown occurs, the True Self can then help guide the Ego Self toward achieving more clarity. In this transaction, the True Self employed what we call "mental Jujitsu." In other words, it disarmed the Ego Self not by protecting itself, but by becoming empty or transparent so the Ego Self had nowhere to go but to open up and speak its pain. Notice that the Ego Self initially began by using a parental tone, and when it got stuck it used the hurt child tone.

The second technique is much simpler and less sophisticated. It requires that the person simply ask to speak first to the parent and then to the child. It is important to follow in this order as the Ego Self uses the parent tone to protect the child. Here is another example:

> True Self: *You are a strong protector; may I have your permission to speak to the Hurt Child?*
> Ego Self: *What for? Who are you anyway?*
> TS: *I mean you no harm; I only want to listen.*
> ES: *Why?*
> TS: *Why not?*
> ES: *OK, but if I suspect anything negative the interview is over!*
> TS: *Of course. Am I speaking to the hurt child?*
> ES: *Yes.*
> TS: *How are you feeling?*
> ES: *Afraid.*
> TS: *I am afraid sometimes too. What are you afraid of?*

At this point the True Self tries to discover a specific strong feeling and then query as to the strong thought that created it in the first place. The person playing the part of the True Self can begin to use a more advanced technique like the ones you will learn about later on.

Model 4: The Transpersonal Model

The next model comes from a transpersonal[9] view of the self. Some of the language is taken directly from depth psychology, much in the same way that I took some of the language for the model of the parent, adult, and child from transactional psychology.

Transpersonal Model of the Psyche

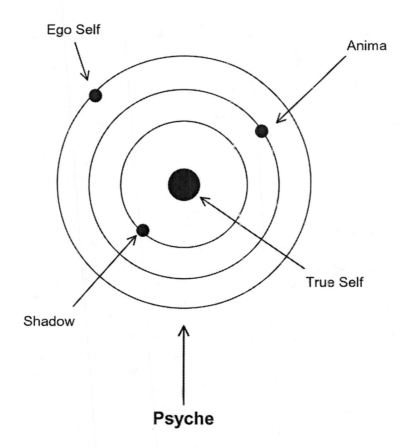

Psyche

The transpersonal model is somewhat like a solar system model of the psyche. In the center of a series of concentric circles lies the True Self, like the sun. The next concentric circle is the Shadow. Beyond the Shadow lies the Anima circle. At the outer edges of the psychic solar system is the orbit of the Ego. The system itself is closed but expanding. Any material in the system cannot be destroyed but can be transformed.

The Transpersonal Model helps us realize that most of the time, when we are in a situation that is causing us difficulty, part of the reason we are unable to be clear about it is that we are literalizing the experience. The model helps explain what I mean. This practice is really about reorientation, just as we talked about at the beginning of the book. The Ego, like those who thought the earth was the center of the universe, often considers itself to be the center, and it looks out beyond its own psychic solar system for meaning rather than looking within to understand and interpret events that are occurring. It looks outside the psychic solar system and into the world of objects to try to interpret and find meaning. The Ego Self, because of its evolutionary orientation, thinks meaning is about the world of doing and having. The inner world of the True Self, because of its time-less nature, knows meaning is about the world of Being.

The circle that is closest to the Ego Self is the Anima, a Latin word that means spirit. The Anima is the part of us that represents our creative energy. It is some-times referred to as libido energy or sexual energy. However, the Anima is more than just sex. It also refers to anything creative that excites and animates us. The Anima is a conduit to the True Self. Things that really turn us on and drive our creativity can be a way for us to connect to our True Self.

The circle closest to the True Self is the Shadow. The Shadow is made up of all the material that gets displaced by the defense mechanisms of our adapted or hurt child, the repressed material our hurt child does not want or does not know how to deal with. This energy has to go somewhere. The Four Directions views the psyche as a closed and growing universe. The Shadow gets all this discarded energy.

Why is the Shadow so close to the True Self? The information discarded to the Shadow, after being brought out in the light of mindfulness, is what ulti-mately gets us into harmony with our True Self. We have been hiding from this secret treasure, afraid to use it and see it for what it is. The Anima contains infor-mation that is much more fun for us to deal with, but it is the Shadow material that we tend to be afraid of because we interpret it literally rather than symboli-cally. The Shadow material should be taken as a metaphor.

For example, Sue thinks, "I hate this person, I wish he were dead." That is a child's thought. Then Sue thinks, "I shouldn't have those feelings." This is a parental thought. Next, Sue begins to think that she is not a good person, even though in reality she really does not wish death on anyone. She just wishes that the unpleasant situation that the person is causing would go away.

Suicidal ideation is based on the same process, wanting the problems to go away but not really wishing to be nonexistent. A person who is depressed may have suicidal thoughts. Those thoughts may not be dangerous and do not necessarily indicate a desire for death, but rather a way to escape the problems. Indeed, from an awakened point of view, suicidal thoughts may metaphorically indicate the need for an old, fixed ego identity to change or die and be reborn as a fresh, more flexible sense of self.

When you realize that most of the information that comes from the Shadow is metaphorical, you will no longer be afraid of it. You can open up and be receptive to the whole thing. Most people are afraid to do that because they do not want to see the ugly or the negative in themselves. Yet often they find that the ugly and the negative are pushing their buttons. The Shadow can turn into a very rich resource of clarity and understanding for reuniting with the True Self.

For Sue this means that she could express empathy for the hurt child within her, without allowing it to dictate her emotions or behavior. It would also mean that she could accept her negative thought about herself as an awkward and unhelpful attempt at asking her to look at the situation differently. Parental admonitions are often inappropriately authoritative. While they intend to help us, they ultimately only reinforce our negative conditioning.

The Anima is most often experienced when a person is not awakened and not turning inward to the True Self. He or she projects that energy onto a person, place, or thing. For example, saying, "Boy, if I only had this person in my life, or this thing, or this situation, then I'd be happy." They project their energy outward rather than focusing it inward to discover what they need to do creatively. When they project this energy onto an object outside of themselves, transference occurs from the ego to the person, place, or thing. In psychology, transference is the process whereby a person unconsciously redirects feelings or emotions onto another person or object.

It is the traumas and dramas of old relationships that are experienced in new ones. I see a lot of this in counseling. Not only do we project our Shadow individually, we also do so collectively. After 9/11 it became very easy for Americans to project their Shadows onto people of Arab descent or people of the Muslim faith. There is also a counter transference that comes back from the external object to the person. Transference is a conditioned reaction. What we really need to do is find out what the Shadow is trying to communicate to us.

Bill and Betty

Let us say Bill is having difficulties with his girlfriend, Betty. He meets a new girl and suddenly feels that he needs to be with this new girl and that he would be much happier with her than he is with Betty. When he thinks about this new girl he gets excited, and all sorts of new thoughts arise. In reality, he has projected his Anima onto this new girl. At one time he did that with Betty, but after a while, projections were all that were left. However, there is a real person there that he is neglecting to see.

Every relationship includes projection and transference. The best relationships, according to the Four Directions, involve a person who is aware of the fact that he/she is almost always projecting. When you are able to recognize that you are projecting, you can then decide to truly love the other person for who he or she really is. You will come to appreciate the person without overvaluing or objectifying him/her and without expecting him/her to carry your entire psychic Anima.

It is unfair for Bill to use this new projection to make decisions about his relationship with Betty, because there is no way Betty can always carry that projection. Nobody can do that for Bill. He must do that for himself. Maybe Bill then comes to someone like me, a counselor. The first thing I would do is to say, "Bill, we realize this new girl is a projection of your Anima. What this situation is trying to say to you is to turn inward, there's something you need to create, there's something you need to look at that you are ignoring. Whether or not your relationship with Betty is something you need to change or reevaluate is another question. Before you can get to that, you have to recognize what is really happening and ask yourself what this situation is trying to teach you."

Exercise 8

This exercise is where the practice of imagination comes in. I often say to a person, "Why don't you talk to the Anima or the Shadow?" Use your dynamic imagination and visualize during meditation. After you have done your calming meditation and you find yourself more centered, speak to the Anima as if it were a person. Ask, "What are you trying to tell me?" Write down the first things that come to your mind. Keep paper and pen or pencil handy when you sit. You can do this with the Shadow also. If you are not afraid of the Shadow, then you can work with it. Remember that the information you receive is metaphorical and not to be used literally or superstitiously. Decoding and interpreting such metaphors can be made clearer with the help of an experienced guide.

Exercise 9

Dreams are a way, like free association, for information from the True Self to be communicated to the Ego Self without interference from the Ego's defenses. For this exercise, say to yourself, "I want to understand myself better and I know that my dreams often communicate to me the things that I need to know." Keep paper and pencil on the nightstand beside your bed. When you wake up from a dream, write it down immediately. If you don't record it immediately, you will likely forget most of it. If you have a hard time remembering your dream, chances are it was not worth remembering. Do not worry about that. If you can recall a dream or a large part of a dream, that indicates there is something there that could be useful.

Write it all out. Then you can go through the dream very carefully. This is very important. Ask every part of the dream, "What are you trying to tell me?" Say there is a blue sky and a brown building in the dream. Ask the blue sky, "What are you trying to tell me? What does the blue sky represent?" You ask the brown building, "What do you represent? What are you trying to tell me?" Ask any individuals in the story what they represent.

Finally, ask yourself, "What part of this dream did I most associate with, and to what part of the dream do I most have an aversion?" Both aspects of the dream can provide a great deal of insight into what is happening in your psyche. Again, the idea is that the psyche is constantly seeking homeostasis and harmony. We say that the True Self is seeking and calling out to the Ego Self, that we are being lured into wholeness. Through the imagination, through the libido, through creativity, through dark energy, our True Self is always trying to bring us to wholeness. There is nothing within us that is going to be cut off. Everything stays. It is just a matter of orientation and understanding.

Summing It Up
The Second Direction: Understanding the Ego Self

- There are three ego states; they are traditionally called the parent, the adult, and the child. The first state, the parent, does not necessarily just represent our biological parents. It represents our whole five-stage historical development. The parent conditioning has two faces. One side of the parent, the yin side, is nurturing. It is very creative, positive, and loving. The other side, the yang, is the critical and destructive aspect of the parent. The child protects itself from this aspect of the parent with defense mechanisms.

- This creates a child with two faces. The key to understanding the child is knowing that the child is the realm of the affective, or emotional, and somatic, or physical, expression of our Being.

- The adult state is the intermediary between the parent and the child. It represents a person who is awake. The adult also has both a yang and yin aspect. The yang aspect is compassion. The adult in us knows how to be empathetic; it knows how to be compassionate. The adult in us also knows how to reason because it has wisdom, the yin aspect. The adult offers compassion toward our own inner child, because that child is not going to be set free until it feels love and safety.

- The True Self always begins with compassion and then moves into wisdom.

- The Transpersonal Model of the Psyche helps us realize that often when we are in a situation that is causing us difficulty, part of the reason why we are unable to find clarity is that we are literalizing the experience. When the Ego considers itself to be the center, it looks out beyond its own psychic solar system and into the world of objects for meaning rather than looking within to understand and interpret events that are occurring. The Ego Self thinks meaning is about the world of doing and having. The inner world of the True Self knows meaning is about the world of Being.

- The Anima is that part of us that represents our creative energy; it is sometimes referred to as libido energy or sexual energy. It does not just refer to sex, but to the creative things that excite and animate us. The Anima is a conduit to the True Self.

- The Shadow is made up of all the material that gets displaced by the defense mechanisms of our hurt child—the repressed material our hurt child does not want or know how to deal with.

The Living Mandala: The Second Direction, Mary

The second story illustrates the sitting practice and how sitting meditation and learning to observe our thoughts, feelings, and sensations are another part of practicing freedom. This is the story of a woman who was referred to me by a doctor friend.

Mary suffered from postpartum depression after giving birth to her second child. It was a very difficult time for her. Not only had she developed depression, but prior to the depression setting in she developed a very severe case of Obsessive Compulsive Disorder (OCD). She had, for the most part, an obsessive thought disorder as opposed to exhibiting a lot of the compulsive behaviors that people sometimes do, like repeatedly washing their hands. Horrible images would appear in her mind whenever she got near her baby. She pictured that by touching her baby, somehow she would hurt it, or it would catch on fire.

Mary knew that this was irrational and that she would never harm her baby, but these thoughts went through her mind over and over again, and she seemed to have no control over them. It was getting to the point where it was paralyzing her. She was no longer able to care for the child. She had to have her sister come to care for the baby, and she became very depressed because she couldn't get control of the problem. The doctor wanted to put her on medication to help with the obsessive thoughts, but she was adamant that she would not do that.

Mary came to me very depressed and suffering greatly from this problem. I explained to her the development of the five stages and how sometimes pregnancy will trigger major hormonal and chemical changes in the body that can cause disorders like OCD. That was obviously the case in her situation. I explained that usually there is some endogenous predisposition to OCD, although without a major change in the chemical balance of the brain, the OCD will not happen. However, an experience such as giving birth can cause chemical changes that will make the disorder become a problem.

As to as these terrible images, I explained that at the heart of the problem—whether a person has to count to six every time he or she goes past a certain door, or if a person has to touch something so many times when going past it, or as in her case, if a person feels that they will hurt someone just by touching them—is negative conditioning. In Mary's case, underlying these terrible images was her poor view of herself and her confusion about her self-esteem. This view was created in her earlier life when she was made to feel like the black sheep of the family and, consequently, thought of herself in a negative fashion. Her obsessive images metaphorically reflected this. I also explained to her that because she was so paralyzed with fear and panic, she would never in reality follow through with these things. They were just obsessive thoughts, not things that she would consciously choose to act on. I explained to her the power of volition and tried to convince her that she would not act contrary to her will.

This helped her. Understanding always helps people a lot. Yet she was still being barraged by these thoughts day in, day out. I began to put her through the stages of practice. When we got to the Second Direction, using the sitting meditation by focusing on the breath or on a mantra, she really seemed to turn the corner. By realizing that she could begin to observe her thoughts, she could just let them be there. Normally she would push them away, which only made them worse, or she would go into them and say, "Why am I having these thoughts? There must be something wrong with me, something terribly wrong."

I said to her, "That's an attachment or an aversion. Aversion happens when we try to push away; that doesn't work. Attachment happens when we go into the thought and start to get more deluded and more distorted." I then told her that what I wanted her to do when these thoughts surfaced was not to push them away. I told her that I wanted her to just experience the thoughts, label them as thoughts, and then go back to her breath or her mantra.

She started doing this twice a day for twenty minutes each time. She discovered that during her sitting periods there were times when she could just let a terrible thought arise in her head and neither push it away nor go into it. She could label it as a thought and associate only with her awareness and not with the troubling image.

Mary began to experience times when she was free from her thoughts. At first, the amount of time was very small, but it became longer and longer. She found that during the day, whenever an obsessive thought surfaced she was able to do the Four Steps of Mindfulness (see Chapter Four). She would simply say to herself, "This is just a negative thought coming from my conditioned self, not my True Self; I can be free and clear of this." Then she would do her meditation, usually a traditional method where she would walk or sit. When the thought was no longer there, she would reaffirm to herself that this practice was working. Mary got to a place where she began to have almost a sense of amusement at the surfacing of these thoughts because she knew that even the most fantastic images had no real power over her.

In about three months time she went from having recorded, by her own account, fifteen to twenty episodes of obsessive thoughts each day to one or two episodes of obsessive thoughts each day. At that point we began to dig deeper into her personal situation so we could uncover the root of why she had such terrible self-esteem. Through these practices we were able to completely rid her of the hurtful thoughts. She was free. I explained to her that at some point her obsessive thoughts might return and they might have a different complexion. I told her that she did not need to view this as something negative, but as something positive. The OCD would be telling her that there is something deep within her thoughts that is unclear or distorted.

The obsessions themselves can be turned inside out and seen as a mindfulness bell to help a person say, "Gee, I'm having an obsessive thought. There must be something going on deep down in my thoughts that I'm not clear about. I will take those out and look at them."

OCD is a terrible disorder. I was also able to convince her to consider using a serotonin medication to help with the chemical imbalance she was experiencing. She experienced complete freedom from the obsessions. It was a very powerful experience for her. I always share this story as a way to explain how the practice of sitting and the practice of labeling our thoughts can be life changing.

When people think OCD is no big deal I explain to them that the disorder can become very severe, even debilitating. Then I tell them that there is a way out of it, a way to freedom, and that one way to freedom is found in these mindfulness practices.

4

The Third Direction: Harnessing the Power of the True Self

The Third Direction is when we really begin to focus on mindfulness or clear-seeing practice. The first two directions are more meditation-oriented, but in the Third Direction we begin to delve into analytical and insight practice. There are no new models to learn, and we can begin to take our practice into our everyday experience.

Exercise 10

For those wanting to explore many ways of practice, the Third Direction can include a lot of techniques; it is constantly evolving through new insights and through the experiences of Four Directions counselors. For *Free Your Mind* I have narrowed the techniques down and we will focus on just a few very effective ones that are easy to learn and use.

The most basic is the Four Steps of Mindfulness. You can use this technique anytime you experience a disturbing emotion or a feeling that becomes very strong. The technique gives you a way to deal with the emotion or feeling at the moment it arises. You can free yourself from the chain of reactions to the thought. You do not have to sabotage yourself and start a whole cascade of offensive negative thinking, feeling, action, and of course, consequences. Remember, all of our practices are about freedom.

Four Steps of Mindfulness

Say to yourself:

1. This negative feeling or thought is coming from my Ego Self, not my True Self.

2. I can be clear and free from these thoughts and feelings.

3. Focus on a meditative practice (or redirect your attention).

4. Take time to reaffirm that this has worked and take refuge in the practices of mindfulness.

Hey Joe!

Joe is walking along when suddenly something jogs a negative memory, and he remembers being bullied as a child. Joe begins to feel very bad and perhaps gets angry or fearful.

The First Step of Mindfulness is for him to recognize that these thoughts and feelings are coming from his conditioned self rather than his clear, true nature of mind. He makes a very lucid distinction that these emotions are not coming from his True Self but rather his conditioned self. This is very important because a person now begins to mindfully disassociate from things that damage him/her. This process is a continuation of what we talked about earlier when you learn not to say, "I am depressed," but rather, "I'm having depressive feelings, but I am not depressed." We begin to dissociate or make a separation between being and having, between being and doing. So Joe says to himself, "I'm OK. I'm just having a painful memory, and my hurt child is expressing itself."

The Second Step of Mindfulness is to affirm that you can be free of your conditioning. You can affirm that with this type of practice, you can see clearly where thoughts are coming from and this inevitably frees you from the negative feelings. So Joe says, "I am no longer a powerless child; I am an empowered adult."

The Third Step of Mindfulness is taking action. There are several ways you can do this. One way is to practice suppression. At this stage you can say to yourself, "I know that this is not coming from my True Self. It's coming from my negative conditioning. I can be free and clear right now. I don't have time to meditate or practice, but I can do that later in the day. I can take this material into my meditation period and figure it out then."

Suppression is temporary. We are temporarily putting something off so we can deal with it at a more appropriate time. If, for some reason, we do not make time to deal with the negative thought, it would then be called repression. At that point the negative thought becomes an obstacle because the psyche is a closed universe. Those energies have to be dealt with at some point. If they are not dealt with, they can become part of the Shadow material of our psyche.

Another way of taking action in the Third Step of Mindfulness is to simply practice walking meditation or sitting meditation by focusing on the breath or mantra. You do not want to push away thoughts or feelings or your aversions to them. You also implement the practice that we started in the Second Direction; it includes observer meditation and enlightened self talk.

The steps build on each other and should be done in this order. If you jump from one to the other, you probably won't have sufficient time to develop efficiency or effectiveness in using the practices. That is why they are called practices. We need to practice them.

In this case, Joe can simply take a time-out to walk or meditate. If he doesn't have an opportunity to do this (in actuality there is always time) he practices suppressing his thoughts and feelings until he can unpack them mindfully during his meditation period. Suppression is a temporary and conscious act; repression is an unconscious and sometimes life-long reaction.

The Fourth Step of Mindfulness comes when you realize that the negative thought or feeling has passed, even if it has only passed a little. It will pass because that is the stabilizing, understanding nature of the mind. No thought or feeling remains constant. There is a continual rising and falling of feelings, thoughts, and sensations.

Once the feeling or thought has passed a little bit, we affirm again that this practice is working. Then we take refuge in it once more. This is another form of affirmation like Step Two, only this time we are affirming that the practice works. This is so important because it is the psyche's job to make demarcations from that experience, to say that this is a different or new way to be. In other words, the psyche begins to unconsciously change along with the conscious direction that we give. We begin to create a subconscious subroutine. Our new subprogram starts to say, "You know that this works." It then begins to convert the way the psyche functions into a much clearer, cleaner, and whole process.

These are the Four Steps of Mindfulness. Using them, Joe experiences a lightness and freedom from his disturbing thoughts. He realizes that he no longer has to be a victim of the past and that any problem that arises can be dealt with by utilizing compassion borne of the wisdom arising from clarity.

Exercise 11

The next technique in the Third Direction is The Four Questions of Mindfulness. This is probably the heart of the practice in terms of mindfulness. You will use it to examine the incidents that bother you. It is a good way to look at whatever you may have temporarily suppressed earlier when doing the Four Steps of Mindfulness.

The Four Questions of Mindfulness method itself is relatively simple, but it does take some practice. The worksheet will help you create a Four Questions chart for examining your feelings and thoughts about specific situations. Let us look at the basic technique and then follow Joe as he works with it in detail.

The Four Questions of Mindfulness

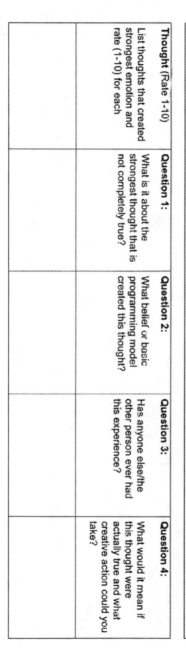

Situation: Write down a paragraph about a situation that keeps coming into your thoughts

Sensation: At least 1 body sensation (sick, skin hot etc.)

Emotion: At least 4 emotions, these will be rated from scale of 1-10 (10 highest)

Emotion	Rating	Emotion	Rating	Emotion	Rating

Thought (Rate 1-10)	**Question 1:**	**Question 2:**	**Question 3:**	**Question 4:**
List thoughts that created strongest emotion and rate (1-10) for each	What is it about the strongest thought that is not completely true?	What belief or basic programming model created this thought?	Has anyone else/the other person ever had this experience?	What would it mean if this thought were actually true and what creative action could you take?

Compile your answers to the Four Questions and create a new and clear thought to challenge the old one. When the exercise is completed take an inventory of how your feelings have changed about the situation.

First, in a few brief sentences describe the situation that bothered you. Note what happened, when, and any bodily sensations (sweating, heart pounding, etc).

Next, write down the feelings and emotions you had about the situation. Were you feeling angry, afraid, anxious, relieved? Then rank these 1-10, with 10 being the strongest. Do this quickly, taking the first number that comes to you.

Now, for the strongest feeling, ask yourself what thoughts created it, and list these in the first column of the chart. Remember, feelings arise from thoughts.

Rate the thoughts 1-10 as to how strong each was. Again, do it quickly. If you take time and ponder it, the Ego Self will kick in and protect itself in making the choices.

Now you will analyze the thoughts using the Four Questions of Mindfulness. Work with the strongest thought first.

Question One: Ask yourself what about that thought is not completely clear or true. Write your answers in the appropriate column.

Question Two: Ask what conditioning or beliefs gave rise to the thought. Write these down.

Question Three: Next ask what is universal about the thought. Is it likely that anyone else has ever felt this way?

Question Four: Now ask yourself what if this thought is true? What does this thought say about you? Write this down.

At the bottom, write your new thought, one that is clearer than the original thought and is a harmonious balance of insight and action.

Finally, ask yourself how you now feel. If you feel the same as you did, or even worse, do the exercise again a bit later. You may find you need to do it several times until clearer thoughts emerge.

Let's work with The Four Questions of Mindfulness method in a specific situation. Joe is checking out at a supermarket when he sees a person that he used to be romantically involved with. This triggers a troubling memory. He remembers their painful breakup. At that point he should practice the Four Steps of Mindfulness because he cannot do anything further about the situation at that moment. Later in the day, when Joe sits down to his evening meditation he can take out his journal and write down the particulars of the incident following the Four Questions of Mindfulness.

He begins by describing the situation as simply and distinctly as he can. It is important to be specific about when the situation took place because sometimes patterns develop. There may be certain times of the day or certain types of associations that tend to trigger negative thoughts and feelings. You then realize that you can begin to avoid those or begin to work around them more creatively.

For example, Joe notices that many of his disquieting moods occur in the evening. This tells him that he shouldn't be doing anything stressful in the evening, and he needs to rework his schedule so he is able to relax during the evening instead of dwelling on problems. He needs to shift problem-solving activities to the morning or afternoon.

Next, Joe asks himself, "What was the feeling you noticed?" He uses mindfulness to help orient or bring himself back, to help him be aware of what was going on. He records his feelings. "How did I feel physically at that moment?" Joe writes down if he felt flushed or uncomfortable, angry, sad, or confused. Recording those feelings and emotions brings the left hemisphere of the brain into play.

Now Joe numbers each feeling from one to ten in terms of its intensity to determine which feeling bothers him the most. Once again it is important for him to do free associations with the numbers. Joe picks the first number that pops into his head. This allows him quickly to locate the root of what is bothering him.

When he finds out which feeling is most intense, he can begin to work with it. Something unique about mindfulness is that it has a domino effect. If you can locate and deal with the root feeling, the others usually clear up by themselves. If a feeling rates less than a five, it is not usually strong enough to worry about.

Joe finds that anger is his strongest feeling. He then writes down the thoughts that are driving the anger. Remember, we know that it is impossible for the feeling to occur without there first being a thought. The source of the feeling was the thought that caused that feeling. Joe numbers each of the thoughts from one to ten to find out which thought was the strongest. Now we can determine the root cause.

What we usually find in a situation like this is that the thought is significant in two ways. Let us say that the strongest thought driving Joe's anger was that the person in the supermarket situation really made him feel like a loser. What inevitably comes out is that in some fashion Joe is saying something negative about his own being. In this case, Joe says the main thought driving his anger is that this person represents everything that is wrong with his own life. What does that mean to Joe? To Joe, this means that he is terrible at relationships and probably deserves to be alone. His being is under attack. He ranks this first. This state is so strong in him because he believes this is saying something fundamental about his being.

Next he challenges that thought with mindfulness. He asks himself Question One: Is there anything about the thought "I'm a loser" that is not true? What distortions or delusions might there be in that thought? For one thing, his relationship issues are about doing and having; they're not a statement about his being. His ability to be in a good relationship is an ego skill which he can work to improve, but he cannot improve or detract from his True Nature. That is the first distortion or delusion.

One of the things we find in mindfulness practice is that 99 percent of the time the situation is not really about us personally. It is likely that many of the situations you assumed were about you actually have nothing to do with you. For example, Joe is not even sure that his difficulties with his past lovers were really just about him. The reality of the situation is that it takes both people to make a relationship work or fail.

In Question Two we ask what sort of conditioning leads to these false thoughts. We can look to the models to see their conditioned origin. For example, Joe realizes that his thoughts are coming from his critical inner parent, and his feeling of anger is coming from his hurt inner child. Together they form his adaptive conditioning which causes him to blame himself for everything.

In Question Three, we need to take the ego out of the equation and ask ourselves, is there something about the thought, "I'm a loser" that we all can relate to? In other words, if I asked a dozen random people on the street if they had ever had an experience that made them feel that they were a loser, is it possible that the majority of those people might say, "yes?" Of course it is. This question is like a mirror that reflects the thought that takes us out of the egocentric realm and makes it more universal.

Question Four, the next part of this exercise, is the most difficult, but working with it also can be the most freeing. What does the thought say about me? What does it mean if it is true? Where do I go from there? This is really the heart of the practice: looking clearly at a situation and making a choice about what to do. Joe tells himself that everyone feels like a loser at some time, and that is OK. Sometimes, for no apparent reason, people just do not like you. It's an experience we all have and it is OK. We do not need to have everyone like us to feel happy. Sometimes you go into a situation and discover that you are reminded of a past event in which you were unsuccessful and then you project that on to a new person.

Once you've completed Question Four, you can put the concepts together to form a new, harmonious thought comprised of your reflections. In our example, we know what Joe went through, and we realize that everybody has had an experience that made them feel like a failure. But the truth is that our success or failure is not something that we accomplish alone. It is always a joint venture.

The truth is that everyone has felt like a loser at one time or another; this is a universal experience. In this particular case, Joe did not even know for sure whether the person was still upset or not.

After he has put those insights together he will form new, clear thoughts that will challenge the old ones. When he looks at the harmonious thought he can then ask himself, "How much do I believe that this thought is a reflection of just the way things are?" Note that we do not have him ask himself to reveal the way he wishes things were, nor do we ask him to list the way he wishes things were not. We only want him to consider a mirror of reality. Then we use the one-to-ten numbering system again, with ten representing total reality. In most cases, Joe is going to find that the harmony thought is pretty close to reality. If it is not a ten, it's at least a nine. When he looks back at his old thought and asks himself how much that old thought represents reality, it becomes easy to see that the number is very low. It probably rates a two, and Joe can now see that it reflected his feelings more than it reflected reality.

Joe can now ask himself if he feels worse, the same, or a little bit better after having done the exercise. Even if he feels only a tiny bit better, it is important that he recognizes that. Clarifying his thoughts will always clarify his feelings. Joe might have to come back to the situation and the exercise more than once. If he feels only slightly better, he can do it again later. Usually by the second or third time he will notice a shift and feel considerably better.

The Four Questions of Mindfulness method is very simple, but it is important for you to ask all of the above questions about yourself. It is important to take the time to go through the process. If you fail to do so, you do not get its full benefit. The more you do it and the more you take time to go through it, the more you realize, "Wow, this really works." Then implement the exercise with each new instance that arises. It will begin to come naturally, as you will have made it a familiar path through practice.

I recommend that you keep a journal of your reflections. Writing or talking about your thoughts really changes the way the brain processes them. Keeping a journal is similar to creating a subroutine. It also allows you to go back over time and see how you have been progressing. When people look back at a year of journal entries, back to a time when they were in the deep throes of depression or anxiety, most are shocked that they believed those unclear thoughts and felt and behaved out of them!

Summing It Up
The Third Direction: Harnessing the Power of the True Self

- The Third Direction is when we really begin to focus on mindfulness or clear-seeing practice. The first two directions are more meditation oriented, but the Third Direction is where we begin to get into analytical and insight practice.

- The Four Steps of Mindfulness can be used anytime you experience a disquieting emotion or feeling that becomes very strong. The Four Steps are:

    1. This negative feeling or thought is coming from my ego self, not my true self.

    2. I can be clear and free from these thoughts and feelings.

    3. Focus on a meditative practice.

    4. Take time to reaffirm and take refuge in the practices of mindfulness.

- The Four Questions of Mindfulness method is:

    1. Write down the troubling situation.

    2. Write down the feelings associated with the situation. Rate their strength from 1-10.

    3. Write down the thoughts that created the most disturbing emotion. Rate their strength 1-10.

    4. Analyze the strongest thoughts by asking the Four Questions: What about this thought is not completely clear or true? What are the conditioned origins of this thought? What is universal about this thought? What does this thought say about me?

    5. Create a new thought that is clearer than the original thought.

    6. Evaluate how this exercise has changed your feelings about the situation.

The Living Mandala: The Third Direction, Jimmy

The third story illustrates the power of mindfulness as used analytically in the Third Direction. You look at the situation that creates negative feelings, delve into the thoughts that create the negative feelings, then question or challenge those thoughts with mindfulness. Through this we can see if thoughts are distorted, and we can try to develop a clearer thought process.

The story I like to share about this concerns a fellow I worked with in a federal prison some years ago. I was running a meditation and counseling group for men imprisoned for various reasons, from stealing, to drug dealing, to assault. One fellow in particular, Jim, had actually committed rape twice and had mugged and assaulted several people.

I was teaching them the practices. We got to the point where we began talking about mindfulness, and we began to go through the thoughts. I explained that sometimes we will look at a thought and take ourselves out of it. I then asked if anybody had had an experience like this. I asked if anyone had tried to be less egocentric in order to see through the eyes of other people, thus understanding our interrelatedness and interconnectedness.

Jim, who was normally very quiet, spoke out and said, "You know Sensei Stultz, I have to tell you that I have never personally experienced remorse for what I have done."

I asked, "Could you explain more what you mean?"

He replied, "As I'm sitting around here listening to this group and listening to people talk about what they did and how they feel bad about what they did, I have to tell you that I do not have any bad feelings about what I did. I remember very clearly beating up some guy and robbing him. Then I had a milkshake and a sandwich and never thought twice about it. In fact, some people label me a sociopath because I'm not able to feel bad about the things that I do."

I continued, "OK. Let's just assume that you aren't able to feel remorse. Let's assume that either because of your genetics or because of some experience that occurred in your early life you really can't experience a negative or bad feeling. The good news from the Buddhist point of view is that you don't need to feel badly in order to act in an ethical way."

I then said, "Let me illustrate this. Will you put your chair in the center of the group please?"

He put his chair in the center, and I directed, pointing to the other inmates, "We are going to stand around Jim. Each of you pick up your chair." Everybody did that.

"On my command, one at a time, take turns hitting Jim over the head with your chairs."

He looked at me and stated, "That's crazy!"

I asked, "What's the matter?"

He responded, "Are you serious?"

I said again, "We are all going to take turns smacking Jim in the head with chairs as hard as we can."

He exclaimed, "You're crazy!"

I replied, "What's wrong; I don't understand what the problem is?"

Jim said forcefully, "I don't want to be hit in the head with the fucking chairs."

I told the other guys, "OK, you can all sit back down. You can move your chairs back to the group setting, and we will talk about this." Jim too returned his chair to its original location, and he sat down.

I explained, "You see, Jim, the reason I did this was to illustrate that even though you may not be able to feel with what people call a conscience, you knew that if we all hit you with our chairs, you would feel pain. Even if you were not fearful at that moment, you knew that being hit by the chairs was going to hurt. This knowledge and awareness of the pain you would experience upset you. Is that not true?"

He said, "Yeah, of course."

I continued, "Now here's the point. Those people you robbed and raped—you don't have to feel anything to know your actions harmed them."

Jim just stared at me. He didn't say a word. He did not have to feel anything to know that he did not want to be beaten up. You could see the light of awareness ignite in his eyes. He said, "I never thought about it that way. I was always just focused on the fact that I didn't have negative feelings about it."

I replied, "Jim, I know it's very easy to put labels on people such as 'sociopath,' and I know it's easy to say there is something wrong with people if they are impulsive and without any feelings. Maybe on a chemical level this is true, but here's the point: to practice non-harming you don't have to feel anything. The virtue of the Four Directions practice is that you don't have to have a strong feeling in order to not harm someone or to help someone."

In other words, for me to show someone compassion doesn't mean that I have to like a person, hang around him, or feel good about him. In fact, I could dislike the person, but I recognize that none of us wants to suffer. I can be compassionate towards him without liking him. That's the beauty of this whole thing.

Jim got it. After that experience, some of the guards commented that Jim seemed like a new person. That's the power of mindfulness. It can come in many ways. It can come by simply challenging our thoughts, or it can come by allowing us to see things more clearly and understand relationships more honestly. We are not basing what we do or what we don't do on our feelings. Rather we base our actions on clarity. In this case, the clarity of interdependence helped Jim realize that harming others is not in harmony with the deeper, symbiotic meaning of life.

5

The Fourth Direction: Trusting in the True Self

The last Direction is related to the first. It is probably both the easiest and in some ways the most difficult. The last step is cultivating faith or trust in the idea of the True Self within us. Through practicing the first three Directions, you will realize that there is a great advantage to the practice of mindfulness and understanding the dynamic of the True Self/Ego Self relationship. By learning to distinguish between the self-confidence issues of the ego and the inherent nature of your self-worth, you can begin to more freely explore your ego issues and make the changes that bring about a joyful experience of being.

Whether you believe the True Self exists or not, orienting yourself this way and adopting the philosophy of finding your self-worth inherently without basing it on doing and having is incredibly practical and frees you up. You are feeling better, but taking the next step of starting to rely on the True Self is what the Fourth Direction is all about.

There are two ways to go about the practice of cultivating this awakened heart or trust. I put these two practices together into a very simple form. Essentially, you begin to see the True Self as more than a pragmatic philosophy. It is no longer seen as an experiment, neither is it a way to approach things just analytically. You see it as something real, something that has always been there, something that is there in an infinite, ancient way, and you see it as something that will always be available to you. This allows the Ego Self to relax into its embrace. Sometimes it is as simple as just saying, "I don't know what to do, please help me, True Self."

The positive affirmation practice is also very powerful. Again, using the imagination, allow your Ego Self to have a conversational relationship with the True Self. Allow the Ego Self to openly express its fears and its desires to the True Self.

Allow that child part of you to completely let go and express itself. Then say an affirmation.

One of the affirmations that we use at the House of Meditation (the name of our Buddhist centers) is, "Breath by breath, trusting in the True Nature of Being, every world is my world." This verse helps us realize that when we experience great change, the new world we find ourselves in may seem alien or foreign. We need to affirm that we are always connected and that we always belong, all of us alone as individuals, living together.

What you will find in the True Self, and this is how you will know it is the True Self, is that there is always compassion expressed first. The True Self responds spontaneously with compassion. Remember the model about the parent, the adult, and the child? Compassion is coming from the adult via the True Self. When we communicate with the True Self, saying, "Oh, I'm just so afraid this is going to happen" or, "Man, I really want this to happen," the first thing that we experience is compassion. When we feel that compassion coming through ourselves, then we know we are in touch with our True Self, our True Nature.

If your dialogue becomes critical or offers specific information immediately, it is not coming from your True Self. The first thing we should receive from our True Self is compassion. This also shows us that this is the best way to communicate with other people; we should first be compassionate. Without that compassion, people are not going to be open to anything we have to offer in terms of reason or wisdom.

The second way we can practice living from the True Self is to simply begin to trust it to take care of things. Listen to your True Self, your inner creative intelligence, take it seriously, stay faithful to it, and approach it with honesty. In both good and bad situations, the True Self knows how to deal with anything. We have to cultivate and learn to trust it.

The True Self is cultivated in little ways. It is very helpful to begin by working through an issue or a problem with the help of a Four Directions Mindfulness Counselor. At first you view trusting the True Self as just a useful idea. Eventually you begin to see that it is something you can rely on. Part of trusting is practicing what is called the wisdom of Not Knowing. You can stop viewing the unknown as something negative. The reality that we all live in is that we really do not know anything for certain. By consciously entering into that Not Knowing, with trust in our True Self, we can have the courage to be patient and to continue to persevere. We find that we begin to see that there are only solutions, and that those solutions are only going to come from our True Self. I call this process lucid clarification.[10]

Susie

Susie is fifty years old, a successful realtor with a grown child in college. One day, not long after her daughter has left for her first semester of school, she realizes that the man she has been married to for the past twenty-five years doesn't really respect her. To deal with this situation, she may end the relationship or try to quickly move on to another relationship, only to find that she faces the same problems with a different partner. This is because wherever you go, you often just carry the same issues into a different environment. Susie could instead practice Not Knowing, take a time-out, and work creatively on her own personal issues. Then, only after she feels she has gained some real insight should she make a decision about her current relationship.

It may take time to find the solution, but cultivating the Fourth Direction—nurturing reliance in the True Self—is probably the most powerful thing we can do. Once we master it, all of the other practices seem easier.

Exercise 12

Once you really understand trusting in the True Self purely and clearly, the other practices of mindfulness become more effortless. Your practice of meditation and mindfulness changes from technical problem solving into a beautiful and enriching experience. Sitting meditation becomes a pronouncement that your Being is the ground of your worth. You can just sit there. You do not have to do anything. You can just be, and you can embrace the mystery of being. You just figuratively plant a flag in the ground symbolizing, "My being is enough, and I don't have to do anything to prove my worth." Mindfulness becomes a way to open up to new depths of joy, understanding and happiness. You realize that we are all interconnected in a way that we can never fully appreciate when we focus only on our own problems.

Together the Four Directions move in a circle going into the center and back out; it's an ongoing process. This is the way we move through our lives. Eventually, as we go through the five stages we find we can integrate and move into harmony with each of them.

This might take some time. In the Four Directions, there is the sense that we really do have time. We practice, and we reawaken. Patience and perseverance are part of the practice. If we do not get it now, we will get it later. This is combined with a commitment to do the practices now as in the admonition, "Time is fleeting. Do not hold back. Appreciate this precious life."

The initial problem that brings us to the practices does not usually take long to resolve. However, working through the five stages, or aggregates, can take awhile. The practice becomes more about the joy of understanding and the happiness that comes from clarity than just about a useful means for solving problems.

Summing It Up
The Fourth Direction: Trusting in the True Self

- The last Direction is cultivating faith or trust in the idea of the True Self. By learning to distinguish between the self-confidence issues of the ego and the inherent nature of our self-worth, we can begin to more freely explore our ego issues and make the changes that bring about a joyful experience of being.

- When your inner dialogue becomes critical or gives specific information immediately, it is not coming from your True Self. The first thing we should receive from our True Self is compassion. This also shows us that this is the best way to communicate with other people. We should first be compassionate with them.

- The second way we can practice living from the True Self is to simply begin to trust it to take care of things. Part of this way of life is practicing what is called the wisdom of "Not Knowing." We stop viewing the unknown as something negative. The reality that we all live with is that we really don't know what the next moment holds for us. By consciously entering into that Not Knowing with trust in our True Self, we can have the courage to be patient and to continue to persevere. This is a process of lucid clarification.

- Mindfulness becomes a way to open up to new depths of joy, understanding, and happiness. We realize that we are all interconnected in ways that we can never fully appreciate when we are just focusing on our own problems.

The Living Mandala: The Fourth Direction, Tony and Christine

The fourth story illustrates the Fourth Direction: cultivating faith or trust in the True Self. This story is also related to the first three directions. The first three directions are really about cultivating a mind that is always ready to see past perceptions to practice what is called "Not Knowing."

The last practice is about faith. It is about developing faith in the True Self and trusting in the True Self. We must bear witness to our True Nature. This practice is sometimes referred to as both the easiest and the hardest practice. It is so simple that it can be deceivingly difficult.

Recall the practices of Mindfulness Affirmations and Just Being, which help each of us to live with an awakened heart. We open up to our fears, desires, and anger and are able to express them, embraced by the safe harbor of compassion and wisdom.

The story that I use to illustrate the Fourth Direction is a recent experience of mine. It has to do with grieving the loss of my sister, Christine. Her untimely death has been one of the most difficult things I have had to deal with in my adult life. What was significant for me, in terms of my practice, was that this experience caused me to realize several things.

I remember being with my sister in the hospital where she lay in a coma, her head having been severely injured in a car accident. I would sit in the room and meditate. Sometimes I would chant and then say, "If there's any possible way, please, please let her recover. Please don't let her die. Please let everything be OK." Then I would return to the chanting.

I didn't ask myself why this had happened because one of the things you learn from the practice is to move beyond asking why. The real questions become, "How?" and "What?" When you ask why, you are totally ignorant of your connection to the rest of life. The week that my sister died there was a major tragedy in India. There was an earthquake. I remember seeing a man on television that had just lost his wife, his children, and his parents all in one day. I remember thinking, "This is a horrible but natural part of the order of things, and nobody needs to ask why."

I also remember being able to express a lot of my feelings of anger, a lot of my feelings of hope, and my fears. I then returned to chanting. Sometimes I'd just sit in silent meditation, and I'd try to match my breath with the respirator. Every time it took a breath, I would take a breath. It was a way of feeling close to my sister and harmonizing with her.

Christine's injuries were too significant, and even though the doctors tried valiantly to save her, they could not. She died.

There were many times immediately after that event when I realized some very deep insights into the nature of pain and suffering. I remember one time, just before Christine passed away, I realized that pain comes in many different sizes and shapes, but the suffering is all the same. I remember sitting in meditation, looking at my arm, and coming to one realization. I could take a match and burn my arm; I could hit it with a hammer; or I could cut it with a knife. Each action would cause a different type of pain, but the suffering I would experience would ultimately be the same. I realized that although I was experiencing a terrible loss, I had suffered just as much over things not nearly as important. The pain was different, but the suffering was the same. At the root of my suffering was my Ego Self.

In the days, weeks, and months that followed Christine's death, I would try to practice different techniques, but none of them seemed to work very well. I was not depressed, but I would go into very deep periods of sadness where I would just weep. I wanted my grieving for Christine to be pure; I wanted to be clear. Many times when I would start to cry about missing her, I would practice mindfulness and realize that there were all kinds of thoughts about my own issues present. I was using the pain caused by my sister's death as an excuse to unload and focus on my own problems. I wanted to miss her and grieve for her honestly and authentically.

At one time I remember driving in my truck when a wall of sadness came down on top of me. I started to cry. I cried out loud and said, "True Self, please help me, I don't know what to do. I don't know how to deal with this. Help me. I know that you will help me." And that was all there was to it. I suddenly realized at that moment that this infinite True Self, the Ground of my Being, was something I could never be separated from, not even by death. I ultimately knew all of my life, all of my loved ones, and all of my experiences were intimately connected in that reality, and therefore, I could never be separated from it. The idea of a separate self is a complete delusion. The truth is that I am deeply interconnected with the universe itself, and this experience I had was not an alien one.

A peace came over me. I realized that no matter what happened in my life I could not be separated from that reality and that the True Self had the resources of radical acceptance, love, compassion, and wisdom that I needed. If I would practice doing what needed to be done while exhibiting the patience to wait for the wisdom to come, I could find the perseverance to keep going and all would be OK. As I went deeper into that experience, all the practices that hadn't been working suddenly began to work as if a switch had been turned on inside of me.

I still deeply love and miss my sister. I miss her every day, but now when I miss her, I really miss her. Those feelings are not tied up with a whole bunch of other things. When I think about her, I don't think about the sadness or about the separation. I think about what her life meant, what kind of person she was, and how devoted she was to others. I think about how she was a teacher to me; I think about her caring and kindness.

6

Coming Full Circle

A practitioner of mindfulness learns that all of the practices flow in an interconnected, ongoing journey around and within the Four Directions, which always lead to and go through the center of our True Self. We can cultivate this relationship to the True Self by simply thinking of the True Self as a part of us, a spiritual power within that we can speak to and be with, a power that knows us and understands us. It is very intimate. By developing a very personal sense of that relationship with our transpersonal True Nature, we can tell it all the things we want, and we can tell it all the things we are afraid of. We can trust that no matter what, wisdom and compassion will be there.

In time, the reorientation becomes complete. The Ego Self is no longer controlled by fear and taking, but has opened up to the free, giving, larger life of the True Self.

I remember one of my teachers saying that there are three basic attitudes: "I can't take this anymore;" "I'm not going to take this anymore;" and the middle way, "I can take anything you throw at me, I can handle anything." The middle way is always initiated by the True Self.

The first and second attitudes come from the hurt child and the angry parent within us. A lot of the not-taking-this-anymore attitude comes from thoughts that are striking out at those above us. The middle way attitude, however, comes from our True Self, the adult, the clear conduit to our True Ground that shows us that we are actually able to handle everything and experience a growing sense of gratitude. When all is said and done, I believe that gratitude is the greatest practice of all.

Endnotes

1. The Navayana School of Buddhism is a new vehicle of awakening in the Buddhist orientation.

2. Liberation is defined here as an individual's process of becoming both free and responsible for defining his or her own life.

3. Sanskrit: refers to a magical circle that conveys the spirit of wholeness.

4. This was created by the Buddha and is also known as the Chain of Dependent Origination. It has been modified by the author to show an individual's psychic historical development.

5. Individuation is the gradual integration and harmonization of the Ego Self through the resolution of successive layers of psychological conflict.

6. One exception to this would be the so-called "instinctive" reaction to danger, otherwise known as the fight-or-flight response. We inherit this hereditary information structure during the first stage of genetic formation. The other exception is the case of the person who is traumatized during the earliest stages of development before they have either memory formation (up to age 3) or cognitive dissonance and context. An example of this would be a child who was molested and then as a young adult becomes either extremely frigid or licentious in behavior.

7. The Precepts in Buddhism are helpful ideas that aid the practitioner.

8. Etymology: to be complete or whole.

9. Transpersonal psychology is a term that is generally applied to Jungian or archetype psychology.

10. Lucid clarification is a term created by the author to refer to the process of practicing mindfulness with specific understanding of the underlying conditioning sources behind our thoughts, feelings, and sensations.

Going Further

If you have found relief from suffering, more freedom, and more happiness through the insights and practices of this book, and would like to take your exploration further, please contact The Blue Mountain Lotus Society (www.bmls.org). You can speak with a Four Directions teacher about private Mindfulness Counseling or perhaps starting a Four Directions Circle in your own area. A Four Directions Circle is a special meditation group that meets regularly to practice together using the Four Directions. A special Four Directions Leader's Guide is available through The Blue Mountain Lotus Society.

If you would be interested in having Sensei Tony speak in your area, please contact him at 717.671.5057.

978-0-595-41953-1
0-595-41953-4

Printed in the United States
78784LV00004B/587

9 780595 419531